GOING OFF THE GRID

The Complete Guide to Your Personal Freedom

Alexander Rejba

TheSmartSurvivalist.com

CONTENTS

DISCLAIMER

INTRODUCTION

How appropriate that this book was written in 2020. I've been researching and experiencing the off-grid life for quite a while now, but in the year of COVID-19, the need to go off the grid is acutely felt on the worldwide level. Now, more than ever, people desire to get away from the unruly crowds and start independent and clean lives.

But before we get any further, allow me to briefly introduce myself. I'm Alexander Rejba. Hiker, survivalist, avid supporter of living off the grid. The book before you is a result of several years of research, interviews with experts and accumulated experience. This book is precisely what you need to get you started on your path to personal freedom and independence. After you're done reading it, you will know exactly how to go and live off the grid.

Before anything, it would be wise to clear some air and define what exactly is meant by "going off the grid". The grid, basically, is your country's power grid. It's huge, expensive and polluting. In a wider sense of the word, "the grid" is the combination of certain negative aspects of today's civilized world. You may love your country and your nation, but it monitors you closely and demands that you use its utilities and power sources. A country can frequently dictate how you live your life, how you work, consume and spend your money. It influences the quality of the air you breathe and of the food you eat. While the country's intentions are probably well-meaning, this is not what a true freedom is.

Once you go off the grid, you produce your own electricity, build a clean and reliable water and sanitation system, and may even grow your own food, without harming planet Earth by your carbon footprint. There is nothing criminal or illegal about the off-grid living. You are not hiding from authorities, you are living your life exactly how a smart, responsible and independent person would. I go into more detail on the legality subject later in the book.

Living off the grid contributes to your well-being on so many levels. You will be breathing fresh air, eating healthy food, exercising while you take care of your new house. You will grow and become stronger – physically, emotionally, mentally, spiritually, you name it. You will fully experience an independent life away from the noisy civilization centers, from their pollution, anxieties, social unrest, and hectic rat race.

And if that's not enough, know that living off the grid will also save you money. Producing your own energy and growing your own plants and livestock are guaranteed to have a positive impact on your budget.

A few words about the flow of this book. The first part deals with preparation. Going off the grid demands preparing, both financially and mentally. The second part surveys the various countries and helps you find the best off-the-grid places within your own country's borders.

Once you have enough information about what it takes to go off the gird and what the best locations are, we will move on to the practical guides and information. I will teach you about alternative sources of energy (solar, wind, water), farming, establishing water and sanitation systems, communicating with the rest of the world, and so on.

The last part deals with different approaches to the off-the-grid living. Did you know that you can also live off the grid in a van, RV, or even in an actual city? I will explain how this can be achieved and what challenges you might encounter.

I'm not a big fan of long introductions, so let's get down to the brass tacks.

PART 1: PREPARATION

PREPARING TO GO OFF THE GRID

Off-grid living demands careful planning and preparation. It's more than just resigning to a cabin in the woods. You can still enjoy the fruits of civilization while being independent of local power grid, but it takes some serious work. True independence requires dedication and maybe some initial investment. Here is a list of items that you need to take care of before going completely off-grid.

Purchase or Build an Off Grid Living Space

Shelter is one of the most basic needs; you need a roof over your head, a place to be, to sleep, to make and store food, and so on. What kind of living space should you get? It depends a lot on your budget and desires.

Tiny House

A tiny house is a small living space, sometimes no larger than a typical living room. It also does not demand a big mortgage that you have to pay for years. While it can be challenging to inhabit a tiny house, it is no more difficult than living in an RV. You will probably have to take a more minimalistic approach to your belongings. On the other hand, a tiny house can be easily relocated. You can effortlessly move it to a different land or community. A supporting and welcoming community is an important factor here, because you can't just sit in a tiny house 24 hours a day.

Cabin

A cabin is a classic off grid dwelling, somewhat reminiscent of a tiny house, but usually more remote. Many proud cabin owners have built their houses by themselves, sometimes using the local wood material. It is a unique achievement that makes you feel like a pioneer. While some use a cabin as a place for summer vacations, a true off-gridder can live there 365 days a year. Many cabin dwellers hunt, fish, farm and gather, literally living off the land. Besides building the cabin, you can also try building your own furniture, kitchen, outhouse, and other additions. It's a true off grid experience!

Shipping Container

A quick living solution, the shipping container does not require cutting down the trees, thus it can even be greener than a cabin. They are already shaped like a house! It requires little adjustment and can be quickly transformed into a comfortable living space. They can be moved with an ease and purchased for less than a tiny house. And for those who are more creative and wish to expand, you can make an entire building by connecting or stacking several containers together.

RV

A recreational vehicle can suit those who want to live on their own while not being tied to a specific spot or address. An RV can be parked, especially in a designed area, and then you drive off in the morning. You don't pay rent or local taxes, but you do have to pay for the gas, of course. You can purchase a fully equipped and self-contained RV and start using it right away (unlike a cabin, which you need to furnish after building it). A good RV should include:

- Living room or dining area
- Sleeping area

- Kitchen (with a fridge and a stove)
- Toilet
- Shower

Naturally, this list is not complete, as you can turn your vehicle into a complete apartment on wheels, with all the luxuries. RVs are costly, but they are a great solution to off grid living space. Find out more about making the off-the-grid RV living possible.

It is also very important to remember that you don't have to actually buy an RV, especially if you need it as a temporary housing solution. Renting an RV is a much cheaper and more affordable option.

I will delve into more details in the part 4 of the book, chapter "Off the Grid RV Living".

Establish a Source of Water

It goes without saying that water is another survival essential. If you don't wish to connect to local utilities, you will need to harvest water on your own. You will need a lot of water in order to drink, bathe and cook, as well as for your farming needs. A simple and cheap solution is placing empty barrels in your backyard, collecting rainwater. A more advanced solution is designing the roof of your house in a stepped or bowl-shaped fashion, so that it collects water effortlessly.

Digging a nearby well or using an existing one is also an interesting option. You can pay someone to drill the well for you. This might set you back a few thousand dollars, but I think it's well worth it! Some terrains are more difficult than others, so the price you will pay for drilling per a foot will vary. Drawing fresh water from a well can meet all your personal and agricultural demands.

I'll discuss the water sources more in the part 3 of the book, chapter "Water Sources and Sanitation".

Learn to Grow Your Own Food

You have a shelter and water, so now let us eat. Our body demands energy, and the off grid living can be a great opportunity to cultivate and grow food in your personal garden. And you definitely have much more land for your disposal, compared to a measly balcony those city slickers have.

If you are not moving around, consider planting perennial plants – they will feed you for years! These can be various bushes, trees and mushroom spots, and you can harvest fruits, berries, nuts and mushrooms throughout the entire year.

And then there are dozens of delicious and nutritious vegetables that you can plant and farm, from seeds or seedlings. Green vegetables, red vegetables, leafy vegetables, root vegetables, a wholesome collection of vitamins and nutrients, clean of chemicals, straight to your table!

If you don't intend to go 100% vegan, you can have chickens and livestock. They will provide you with eggs, meat, milk, and even wool and leather for your clothes, as well as feathers for your pillow.

Another advantage to having your own organic farm is that you can trade and exchange your produce with other members of the community. Therefore, you don't have to grow every possible fruit, vegetable and animal in existence. Instead, grow a few and then barter for the products that your household does not have, or even for other goods and services that you need. An honest barter system, free from currency and governmental supervision.

In addition, you can always try hunting or fishing, or even gathering berries and mushrooms in the forest. Be careful! Study what mushrooms and berries are suitable for consumption. Check what the local laws say about fishing and hunting seasons, do not unnecessarily harm the wildlife in your surrounding area.

I will discuss this topic in more detail in the part 3 of the book, chapter "Farming".

Connect to a Free Energy Source

Living off the grid usually means being independent of the power grid. You collect and produce your own energy. The most common method is the ever popular solar panels. Their installation does not cost a lot, the solar panels have become more accessible and affordable. Solar energy is free and clean, and it makes you 100% off the grid.

You will also need a battery and/or generator for the cloudy and rainy days. Additionally, if you still would like to have the grid option available, there are different types of solar systems that I will explain in the part 3 of the book, chapter "Off Grid VS On Grid Solar".

Alternative energy is the very essence of eco-friendly off-grid living. Moreover, it can save you a lot of money in the long run. The solar panels continue getting cheaper, and they don't demand frequent replacing and fixing. You can expand your solar energy intake by adding more and more panels – just be sure that your current inverter is up to the task.

There is more than one way to use solar energy. You can trap the sun rays with a thermal water heating system, which directs heat to a water tank, providing you with hot water all day long.

You can also try designing your dwelling to make the best use of the sun. It's known as a passive solar design. Use windows, thermal chimneys and thermal masses to cool or warm your house, free of charge and of pollution.

Wind turbine is another excellent energy solution. A large enough turbine can power your entire residence. A small turbine can be utilized to pump the water from the well I've briefly mentioned earlier. Contact a local turbine dealer, explain your needs and get the price offer that suits you.

I will discuss several energy sources in the first four chapters of the part 3 of the book.

Acquire All Necessary Tools and Equipment

While it's nearly impossible to mention all the items that you will need in your new off grid home, here are some of the essentials. The list, naturally, depends on how big your house is and what you plan to do in it and nearby (for instance, whether or not you will have a private garden).

Toolbox

Get one that neatly organizes all the essential maintenance and fixing tools. A toolbox should at least contain: Philips and flat screwdrivers, pliers (preferably with a cutter), adjustable wrench, sink wrench, and a heavy enough hammer. You will also need some supplies, such as nails, bolts, duct tape, glues and so forth. Also, if you can, get a multi-purpose tool, whose versatility earned it a spot on every survival gear list.

Gardening Tools

Shovel, hoe, water hose, shears, rake, gloves, wheelbarrow. You have to own at least these to maintain a healthy and clean vegetable patch. If you have trees, you might also require pruning saw and other similar tools. Becoming a farmer on your own does require some shopping, but these tools are absolutely necessary.

Furniture

Unless you're skilled enough to build your own furniture, you will definitely need to furnish your new abode. A table, a couple of chairs (to sit outside as well) and a bed are the bare minimum that will make you feel like you're in an actual home. But feel free to design even further, turning your tiny house or cabin into a glorious home. Shelves, kitchen, curtains, carpets, you name it. Just because you live off the grid does not mean you have to exist like a Spartan solider.

Kitchen and Food Storage

Whether you're growing food or buying it at the nearby market, your house needs to be equipped with items for food preparation, consumption and preservation. I am talking about the basic utensils, like knives, forks, spoons, plates, pots. Additionally, you must acquire the food preparation tools, like spatula, whisk, tong, ladle, grater, colander, and so on. Just take a look around your ordinary kitchen, anything that you have used more than once should probably be included in your off grid home.

A special attention should be given to food storage. If your garden produces more than you can eat at the moment, your excess food should not be wasted. A small fridge powered from your generator or solar panels is probably enough. Food that does not require cold should be stored in dry, shaded places, preferably in tightly sealed containers and/or a closed cupboard.

Entertainment and Electronic Devices

This one depends on your personal taste. Bring whatever you enjoy for your pastime. It can be books or even a video game console. Unless you intend to completely resign from the mankind, bring a mobile phone (might not get reception in some areas), a laptop or at least a radio. Being off grid does not necessarily mean detaching from the modern technology, but it is not up to me to tell you how to live.

A 3D printer is worth a separate mentioning. When you're remote from the nearest urban center, it's almost impossible to immediately acquire a replacement for a broken part or find an item that you suddenly need. 3D printing can be an answer to such a problem, you can print a workable replacement, at least until you can shop again.

Get Informed Regarding the Local Laws and Limits

Going off the grid is not just about buying the right equipment and growing food. While it could be nice to live in an ideal world where no one bothers you, we are still inside the borders of a country and a nation, governed by people who make all sorts of laws.

So before you move to a cabin, there are certain laws and rules you need to check for that region, county and state. There are building codes that your structure must abide by. There are zoning codes that vary from municipality to municipality, so you must ensure your piece of land follows them. Finding a land that is completely free of codes and property taxes is tricky. Usually it's a spot so removed from the civilization that it would take you hours to get supplies or human help in an emergency.

Local taxes should be taken into consideration while you're figuring out how much budget you will need to live off the grid. In later chapters, I will share more details on laws and taxation related to off-grid living in different parts of the world.

Since it's too challenging (and sometimes illegal) to live off the grid inside a city, your best choice is getting a somewhat rural lot. Again, research beforehand, find out all the possible issues and legalities you are going to face. While going off the grid on a land of your own is legal, it's still worthwhile to see what limitations the local governing body imposes on homesteads just like yours. You might eventually decide to settle somewhere else, if the local government is too restricting.

Another point to check is whether the local authorities are planning future development of the area and how that can impact you. You might enjoy a pristine piece of nature for a while, and then someone builds a polluting factory in your vicinity, or even new suburbs that stretch too close for your taste. Avoid areas with industrial zoning; see what kind of businesses have a permission to build and expand in this particular region.

Speaking of pollution and industrialization, if you plan to situate your cabin or tiny house near a stream – see what's going on upstream. Are there factories, plants or even abandoned mines that carelessly contribute undesired chemicals to the water? This type of pollution is hard to get rid of, no matter how you filter your water.

Prepare Yourself Mentally and Physically

Living off the grid is not an easy decision to make. It requires a certain determined state of mind. You will be moving from a familiar environment, away from the comfort and conveniences of modern life. Everything you will own and eat – you will need to work hard to achieve. Maybe you will join an off grid community, maybe you will live on your own. Whatever the choice is, prepare yourself internally. There are hardships and challenges to overcome, and I'm not talking just about the weather and hunting.

The off grid living is a life-changing experience. You will need to be mentally and emotionally tough. You will also need to be physically prepared, in a good health and shape. You will be doing much more physical work than you're maybe used to. Building, designing, crafting, growing crops, hunting, installing, digging, working – it's a day long activity that requires being fit, ready and full of energy. Make sure you are ready for whatever physical or psychological obstacles are ahead.

THE COST AND EXPENSES

Living off the grid is more than just a trend or a cool expression. It is an actual way of life that many people are drawn to. However, not all of them are aware that such a lifestyle is not about living in the wild, in a cave or a hut. There are real expenses and costs that living off the grid entails.

I have done an extensive research to answer how much it costs to live off the grid. Here is the most detailed information that includes both the initial costs and the day-to-day expenses. Please notice that the numbers mostly pertain to the United States, so check the prices in the country of your interest. Nonetheless, even if you don't live in the USA, you will need to invest in the same items as listed below.

The Initial Cost of Living off the Grid

Let's talk real numbers. There are expenses that you cannot avoid. You need to purchase the land, to establish your off-grid homestead, to get all the systems working. Here is a list of things that you will probably need right from the start. See what applies to you and add the relevant numbers.

Property and Housing

Land

While free lands do exist, you might consider avoiding them. They come with undesirable baggage and conditions, and you will find yourself spending tons of money into making the land livable.

A good lot size for off grid living is 1-5 acres, and in any state this will cost you somewhere between $20,000 and $30,000. If you wish to establish a good garden on your lot, the preferred states for this are:

- New Jersey
- Florida
- California
- Hawaii
- North Carolina
- Texas
- Kentucky
- Missouri
- Arkansas

For further reading on best places to live off the grid in the USA, see part 2 of the book, chapter "USA: Best Places for off Grid Living".

House

Naturally, you will need a shelter. Some lands already have a house that you can inhabit, so you probably should look for those. Lots that weren't developed require more work and preparation, such as making a road, digging foundations, and then building the house itself. You can use your lot's timber as a building material. If you're lucky, maybe some forestry company will clear your lot and pay you for letting them to do so.

So how much will an off-grid shelter cost?

- If you don't have building skills, get a contractor. Almost any American contractor will build you a stick frame house. It will cost you between $120,000 and $150,000.
- If you want a rammed earth house, the price will go up to $200,000.

- If this sounds like a steep price, there are simple manufactured houses that can be bought for $20,000.
- Another option is a cabin, which can be purchased for $50,000.
- An RV seems to be a popular option, especially if you intend to move around once in a while. A second hand motorhome can cost around $10,000 - $20,000.
- Living off grid in a van is another affordable option.
- And finally, if your budget at this point does not allow such an investment, go for the best tent you can purchase. It will cost you somewhere near $500. I have made a list of the best emergency shelters and tents.

Keep in mind that you are just at the beginning of your off-the-gird journey, so maybe a tent or a tiny house is a better choice. Later you can upgrade to a bigger house. I can recommend that you read more on how to prepare for off grid living, especially the part about the living space.

Additional Buildings

Once you have your house built, here are some outbuildings that can be erected nearby – and their costs.

- A **barn** has a multitude of features that affect its price. Height, electricity, tack room, stalls, flooring, temperature control – all these parameters decide how much you will spend on your barn. For instance, a concrete floor is about $6 per square foot. If you decide to build it on your own, it's $10 - $15 per square foot for a pole barn and $8 - $10 per square foot for a steel frame. All in all, a barn costs $10,000 - $20,000 in average.
- A **greenhouse** is a welcome addition to any homestead. There is a small greenhouse available for just $750, which can give your seeds an early start. A bigger setup costs about $10,000, but it provides you with crop all year long. Of course, you can always try build-

ing one on your own.

- **Root cellar** can be successfully utilized to store food. Again, the cost depends on the size. A miniature barrel-like cellar is no more than $100. Larger cellars can cost up to $1,000.
- You can use leftover lumber to build a **chicken coop**. If you prefer to purchase one, the simplest coop costs about $150 and can house up to 4 chickens. A more advanced model is about $1,500.

Energy and Heating

Power Systems

The very meaning of being off the gird is that you are not connected to the power lines. You are not dependent on the nation's power grid, and therefore your carbon footprint is minimized. But you still need your own source of alternative energy. You can go either for a wind turbine or a solar panel. One of those plus an inverter will cost around $1,000. This can be enough to power one refrigerator.

Naturally, you'd want to go for more. You can add more turbines or panels to your system. A regular household will need 5KW power to run. The cost of installing enough solar panels/ wind turbines to reach that goal is $30,000. While this does sound like a lot at first, the system will pay off within 4-20 years. The payoff partially depends on whether or not you receive tax credits. Additionally, in some areas, you can even sell excess electricity back to the local power grid.

Another expense is the batteries. Your free power system will require a backup. A new battery costs $200-$300, so having a complete backup will cost you about $7000. The batteries need to be replaced once in several years. You can also go for used batteries to reduce costs; you can find those at a server farm.

Geothermal Pump

A great way to utilize earth's temperature is by installing a geothermal heat pump. The earth maintains a permanent heat of 50F at the depth of 8 feet. Therefore, a heat exchanger can take that heat and direct it to your house, where you can enjoy a cooler summer or a warmer winter.

To have the exact price for the geothermal pump, you will need to ask a contractor for a quote. Several parameters can change the final price, such as the age of your house, its insulation quality, its size, and how much space there is for the heat exchanging loop field.

Water and Sanitation

Well

Do you need to dig a well? Not if you have a fresh water source on your property. This can be a lake or a stream. Remember that this water must be treated and filtered before you can consume it and use for washing, since it may contain pathogens and chemicals.

If there is no body of water nearby, then your property requires a well, which can be made by drilling into the ground and then installing a pump. The depth of the well affects its cost, since well-digging companies ask for about $15-$100 per foot. A regular well is usually about 100-150 feet deep, which means that the price for the hole drilling can be between $1,500 and $15,000. But that's not the final cost, as you also must pay for the plumbing, electrical work and the pump itself. These add another $800 to $2,000 to the total cost. You will also need a water tank to storage the pumped water in it; it costs about $500 - $1,000.

For those who wish to have several wells, perhaps a cheaper solution will be doing it yourself. Invest $10,000 - $15,000 and purchase a drilling rig. A compact hydraulic rig comes in two versions: stand alone or as an attachment to a tractor/Bobcat.

Grey Water

Grey water system collects your household's used water, such as the water from sinks, shower, dish washer, washing machine, and so on. This water can be reused either to flush the toilets or for the garden. The prices vary according to the system's complexity and the time of its installation (when the house was built or afterwards).

A low cost system is $500 and it reuses the clothes washer's water for the garden's needs. A much more advanced system does an extensive recycling of the grey water by taking it from all the possible sources around the house, filtering it and then storing in a tank. The water stored in the tank can be used for the toilets and the garden. There is more plumbing involved, as well as a pump and the aforementioned tank, which brings the system's cost to over $10,000.

Septic System

A septic system is usually quite cheap. Moreover, with the right maintenance, it can serve you for decades without being replaced. Some factors, however, can bump its price up. For instance, the quality of the soil that will contain the septic system. A soil with a poor drainage ability will raise the price. So when you order the system, mention the soil and ask the contractor to perform a percolation test prior to the installation. This test will determine how well your soil can absorb water.

Also, make a survey of all the local excavation companies and see how many of them are in need of work. Some of them can lower the price if there are not that many customers around.

Check whether you need a permit to install a septic system. Having the right permits is a part of legally living off the grid in the USA.

Composting Toilets

It's possible to recycle human waste by turning it into a fertilizer with the help of a composting toilet. This is similar to the process of turning kitchen scraps to compost. A composting toilet system can transform your solid waste into humanure or humus by using a very small amount of water.

The cost of such a system is approximately $1,900. There is also an option of building a composting toilet system by yourself for no more than $100, one for every bathroom that you have. Alternatively, you can install a centralized unit that attaches to all the toilets and directs the waste into a single composter, for the price of $10,000+. The cost in this case is affected by the volume of waste that the system needs to process.

Farming

Gardening

Let's assume again that you have a family of four. To have enough vegetables for everybody, the garden should cover an area of 4,000 square feet. You can purchase enough seeds for the whole year by spending no more than $100. When the garden starts producing, you can gather the seeds from the plants and use them later to reduce costs.

You will need to invest another $500 - $1,000 for a wire fence, to protect the garden from the foraging animals. The irrigation system is another expense. The cheapest solution would be buying a hose. The more expensive one involves having multiple timers.

Decide ahead what fruits, berries and nuts you wish to grow as well. A tree or a bush can cost from $15 to well over $100. Don't get too excited by all the options, otherwise you'll find yourself spending hundreds of dollars. Find out how every plant grows in your area, how much it produces, and how big it can get.

You can cut down some of the expenses by using compost instead of a fertilizer. Get a bin for the compost, or simply start a pile in the yard. Compost can make your life much easier.

Aquaponics

This is a somewhat advanced ecosystem that combines growing plants and fish in the same watery location. When done right, the fish and vegetables from aquaponics can feed your entire house 365 days a year. Not surprisingly, the cost depends on the size: $500 for a small system and $1,000 for an aquaponics system to feed a family of 4. If you intend to produce enough for the entire year, you'll need a greenhouse around the system (see the costs above). Additional costs include fish food, water testers, electricity, and so forth.

Livestock

If you establish your own mini-farm, then having some animals will vastly improve it. Here are the costs of livestock in off the grid living.

- **Chickens** usually don't cost that much, you can get a few of them for $5 - $10 a bird, plus $2 for a monthly feed for one chicken. One chicken lays enough eggs to feed one person, so at least have as many chickens as there are people living in the household. The chicken live in a chicken coop that I mentioned earlier.
- **Pigs** cost considerably more. If you buy them just for food, their price is anywhere between $15 and $100. 1-2 pigs are enough for a family of 4 to feast on them for a year. Breeding pigs are much more expensive, around $3,000. Add additional $500 for their housing and fence. The food that the pigs eat is around $50 a pig, but you can also feed them with scraps or plants from the garden.
- **Cows'** prices vary between the breeds, and usually they are between $1,000 and $3,000. The meat from one cow can feed a family of 4 for the entire year. Cow's food is up to $200 a month, but you can again reduce the costs by scraps and garden produce. Ideally, a cow will be out there on a pasture. Each cow needs an acre of pasture for itself, providing there is enough

grass. Also, a big pasture requires good fencing, which is a one-time payment of about $2,500. On the other hand, if you keep the cows to milk them, you save money on milk and many dairy products. And if you have a herd, you can have calves for sale or for meat, so your investment is returned to you.

The Daily Costs of Living off the Grid

Now that you have your house running, your garden irrigated and your chicken laying eggs, it's time to mention the costs of a day-to-day life. The off-grid lifestyle requires some additional expenses for the things that you most definitely cannot produce on your own, the total cost of which can run up to $1,000 per month.

- **Household items** are the things that you need to have around the house and that you certainly cannot make by yourself. These can be light bulbs, oil, garden tools, fixing tools, kitchen utensils, plates and pots, batteries, various appliances, and so on.
- **Gasoline**: You need to power your equipment and cars, so you will have to spend money on fuel as well as oil for the vehicles and the machinery.
- **Travel**: Unless you intend to stay on your property 365 days a year, it will be nice to put some money aside for a family trip and vacation.
- **Food**: Not everything can be produced by your mini-farm's plants and animals. Condiments, sugar, salt, soda, oils, yeast – a few bucks will be spent on purchasing all these necessary additions to your food.
- **Healthcare** is a noticeable cost of living. You can save some money on the side for the time of need, or get yourself a good health insurance.
- **Taxes** are unavoidable. Prepare yourself, you will most likely need to pay income tax as well as prop-

erty tax. These, of course, differ from state to state, or whether you live off the grid in the United States or plan to live off the grid in Canada.

- **Insurances** can be optional. However, almost all of the states require that you have to get the auto insurances, and sometimes even the health insurance. Find out about these things before you be surprised by them.
- **Maintenance** is another unavoidable expense. Any of the previously mentioned systems must be taken care of. Worn out parts demand to be replaced, either by your or an expert. Make sure you have put aside money for this expense as well.
- **The Internet** is not a luxury these days, but a necessity. You will probably want to stay connected to the Web, which involves a monthly fee and some initial setup, all of which is covered in a later chapter about off grid Internet.

Reducing the Costs by Living off the Grid

While all the above expenses might sound alarming, you need to keep in mind that the off-grid lifestyle can actually reduce the costs of daily living. Let's list the factors that can positively impact your budget and improve your life.

Energy Costs

The energy costs are rising every year, as the energy companies squeeze another buck from their customers. But since you have moved to live off the grid, you are starting to produce your own energy, either from the sun or the wind, not to mention using the earth's heat to your advantage as well.

Yes, you will need to invest a few thousands of dollars to install the alternative energy systems and to buy the batteries. However, from this point forward, you will not pay any bills sent by the energy company. You are actually starting to save money once your solar panels or wind turbines are hooked to your house. In a few years, the money you have invested into them will be paid off. Not to mention that it's a clean energy, so it won't negatively impact the environment and your health.

Additional way to significantly cut energy costs is purchasing necessary devices - but in their smaller or more portable version. For instance, instead of a huge washing machine consider getting (at least temporarily) a small, portable washing machine.

Healthy Lifestyle Saves Money

The off grid experience greatly improves you, both mentally and physically. Which means saving money on doctors, shrinks and medicine. Here are a few examples how:

- The **food** that you grow and produce is much healthier than anything you can get in a city's supermarket. This is because when you grow it, you use no chemicals and pesticides, the natural way.
- When you run your own farm and homestead, you are **physically active**. You will be much stronger, fitter and healthier. The constant exercise means, once again, that you are spending less money on medical bills.
- **Fresh air** is another terrific factor in favor of your well-being. Nothing can compare to the quality of air in the country.
- **Stress-free life** also has a positive impact on your health. You are no longer living the hectic (and polluted) city life, you live at your own pace, thus reducing stress that negatively affects your body.

Making More Than Wasting

Thanks to the off grid lifestyle, the consumerist habits are no longer necessary. When we are "on the grid", we consume a lot without making anything. We mindlessly spend resources and produce waste. However, once you move to a land of your own, you will start appreciating everything that you make. No money will be wasted on unnecessary products.

Moreover, you will start recycling regularly, which means saving even more money on water and fertilizers. The off grid life is renewable and sustainable. Eventually, your garden and livestock will produce more than you can consume, and you can sell the produce or barter it for other goods.

Community

Speaking of bartering, you will probably get to know a few good people in your community. They can help you save even more money by providing essential knowledge and information about this area, its markets, stores, best deals, contractors, regulations, and so on. Furthermore, you can exchange goods with them, forgoing the use of currency. A happy and positive community is a true treasure. I created a list of off-the-grid communities in the world, feel free to choose one.

Better Control of Your Life

The off gird life offers much better control of your life, your time and your finances. Your mindset is firm and clear, you have the best possible view of what you are doing on a daily basis, how much you need to spend and how much you can earn.

The benefits, of course, go even beyond the monetary expenses and savings. Families bond and grow stronger. The relationships improve and last. Friendships and community become a great source of joy and support. The urban toxicity is left behind and forgotten.

Once you have better control of your time, you can dedicate some of it to creative work. Reawaken old talents or find a few new ones. You probably did not have time for these before moving to the country.

You now also have time to fully appreciate nature, its beauty, its plants, animals, resources. Nature calms you down and makes you focused, reducing all that stress, cleansing your body's systems.

This life is also much safer than the one you had in the urban environment. You don't need to buy a self-defense weapon to carry at all times. This is the safest place to raise a family.

All in all, understand how flexible your life becomes. You are no longer a slave to the urban life's rhythm and circumstances. You are in full control of what you do, when you do it, and how much you spend.

In Conclusion

As you can see, living off the grid is far from free. The total cost of purchasing a lot and building a functioning house can be near $100,000 or even more. But don't let this deter you from realizing your dreams. Once you've settled and established your garden or farm, the investment will eventually pay off and you can fully enjoy your rediscovered freedom. In the long run, you will save more and spend less, while enjoying the best life you can possibly have.

PART 2: OFF GRID LIVING AROUND THE GLOBE

USA: IS IT LEGAL?

Now that we discussed what it takes to start living off the grid, let's take a look at potential countries and locations, starting from the United States of America.

From time to time you might hear rumor or see a news piece about someone being fined or prohibited from living in an off-the-grid home. However, in most of these cases, the reason is not the off grid living itself. To live off the grid is perfectly legal, it goes hand in hand with the American principle of personal freedom. If someone had been prosecuted for living off the grid, it's usually for one or more of the following reasons.

Avoid the Following Choices

Failing to Pay Taxes

This is quite simple and basic: every able citizen must pay taxes. If you own a property, then you have to pay property taxes. Your off-the-grid lot, as secluded and remote as it may be, must pay taxes according to the regulations of the state it's in.

If you are producing crops, livestock, providing services, crafting items, then you must pay taxes as well. Every income is taxable. Naturally, you can check with an accountant whether you are illegible for tax deduction.

To put it bluntly – don't play games with the IRS. Live off the grid freely, without worrying about the taxman's retribution.

Squatting

I mentioned property earlier. People who live off the grid usually buy a land and built their own house. The prices vary between states, I covered this topic in the previous chapter about the cost of living off the grid.

However, some folks have an idea that being off the grid should be something borderline criminal. They squat in nearly abandoned buildings and take over lots that do not belong to them. And when the police comes to evacuate them, they protest that their freedom is being trampled.

This is definitely not the correct way to live off the grid. Again, you need a peace of mind. You will have enough worries with your produce, the solar panel installation, the off grid Internet, and so forth. Simply don't squat. Establish your own property, your off-the-grid lawful kingdom.

Building Codes and Zoning Restrictions

Let's assume you have your own land. Just setting up a tent on your land is not enough. You cannot camp for more than 2 weeks, even on your own land. You can try getting a permit for a longer camping, but it can be next to impossible.

Once you decide to build a permanent house, there are few things to remember in order to avoid butting heads with the law.

- **Minimal footage**: Your tiny house or cabin cannot be too tiny. A minimal square footage must be met, otherwise the local authorities will not permit you to build on your lot. In some counties, the footage must be between 500 to 1000 square feet.
- **Building codes**: You cannot build your house any way you want to. There is a list of international and national building codes that you simply have to follow. It's for your own safety, too. Your building will be inspected, and you can get fined (or worse) if it's not up to the codes. Get yourself familiar with The International Building Code, or hire a building contractor who knows what he's doing.

- **Water source**: Your building must have an access to water, in order to be fully approved. If you're not connected to the water pipes, then you must find another solution. Digging a well or buying a lot with a natural spring are always nice options. Collecting rainwater can be problematic, not every state or county allows this. You should check the local restrictions before deciding on the way you get water to your new property.
- **Energy production**: Fundamentally, you are free to produce your own energy. Some people even sell the surplus to the local power network. However, I suggest doing some research of your own and finding out any unusual restrictions that a local government can invoke.

Septic Systems

Sewage disposal is a significant issue that an off-gridder faces. You cannot dump your sewage anywhere you wish, it's completely illegal and harmful to the environment. And since you are off the gird, you are probably not connected to the nearest town's sewage pipes.

You will need to establish your own septic system, bury the septic tank and have the appropriate permit for the entire setup. While it sounds bureaucratic, the reasoning behind the permit is keeping the environment clean. For the same reason, a composting toilet needs to be approved as well.

Fishing and Hunting Permits

If hunting and/or fishing are a part of your weekly routine, then you must have a permit, even if you are hunting on your own lot. Poaching is definitely illegal. Certain animals are allowed to be hunted only during certain seasons, to keep their population steady. Besides, you moved away from the city to be in harmony with the Mother Nature, right? Not to carelessly rob her of all the resources.

What U.S. States Support off the Grid Living?

Here are a few outstanding examples:

- **Colorado** has become one of the most welcoming U.S. states. The state made sure that the zoning codes are more flexible. Furthermore, quite a few counties are actually building green and sustainable houses.
- **Florida** is known for its legality of off-the-grid living. The lenient rules and laws encourage installing solar and wind energy sources, as well as expanding your homesteads to add a garden or a miniature farm.
- **Hawaii** is already mostly off the grid, the only thing you need to do is to move away from the city. The climate there is a healthy mixture of sun and rains, which creates a fertile soil as well as suitable conditions for off grid living.
- **Missouri** actively supports and encourages off-the-grid settlement. There are no local laws that insist on connecting to a septic system or prevent you from collecting rainwater. The Missouri authorities do not closely regulate an individual's life, and you can live as free from the general society as possible. Another advantage is the local weather that helps growing beautiful and rich crops.
- **Ohio** is quite friendly to off-the-grid life style. There are tons of favorable factors, such as low property taxes, low land prices, low living costs and low crime rates. Many counties don't even have a permit office or strict zoning codes. Add to this plentiful natural resources, and you got yourself an excellent state to live off the grid.
- **Alaska** has very lenient laws and minimal regulation, as far as establishing your off-the-grid homestead

goes. Read more on living off the grid in Alaska.

There are more states that support off the grid living, I will list them in the following chapter.

USA: BEST PLACES FOR OFF GRID LIVING

To answer this complicated question, I've done an extensive research and made a list of the best states and places in the USA that are suited for your off-grid dreams. I will also mention a few good off-grid communities and talk more about the factors that should help your final decision regarding where to move.

15 Best States to Life off the Grid in the USA

Arizona

Specifically, the northern part of Arizona. The land cost is low, and the climate is comfortable. The biggest issue is water, it's somewhat scarce. You will have to transport water to your homestead, or even better – purchase a lot with a water source. If there is water underground, then build a well.

Northern Arizona's long growing season and abundance of sun will definitely boost your crops. The extended sunny periods will also provide you with a free solar energy all year long.

California

The northern part of California is the one I highly recommend. Low land prices and low taxes, abundant water, more lenient laws plus temperate weather equals an awesome choice to live off the grid. The southern half is not bad either, but the land prices are steep and the population density is too high.

An example of a great Californian off-the-grid community is Emerald Earth in Mendocino County. It's actually one big house with about 12 people living in it. They use a composting outhouse, so they are free from the state's sewage system.

Colorado

Colorado is steadily becoming a more welcoming state for those who wish to live off the grid. The codes are getting more flexible, and sustainable buildings are being constructed in several counties. You would have to find a good solution for the water supply, since a large part of Colorado is a desert land. Try looking for a lot away from the cities, and you will find that the land costs less there.

Florida

Florida is an outstanding off-the-grid choice! As long as you have a good water source and septic system, you will be left alone. Unlike the false rumors on the Internet, **living off the gird in Florida is completely legal**.

In Florida, you are free to install whatever alternative energy source and home addition you desire, be it a well, a garden, wind turbines, solar panels system, and so forth. You can raise your own livestock – pigs, cows, hens and roosters, you name it. Preparing to live off the grid is so much easier in Florida.

The rural land is reasonably priced, and there is a lot of water and timber that can be found nearby. You won't find rock though, since most of Florida is soil or sand. However, if you settle down in the south of the state, there are fossilized coral beds that are extraordinarily tough and can be used instead of your regular rock.

Hawaii

The cost of moving to Hawaii could be very high, but it's well worth it. If you're seeking complete independence, away from the main land, then this is the right kind of haven for you. You literally cannot be on the grid, because the grid does not extend further than the city limits. Most of the island is simply off the grid.

Add to this the fact that you have a nutrient-rich soil, generous sun and rains, sustainable energy – and **you can build here your perfect homestead**! You can grow almost anything here, even coffee beans (which cannot be grown in any other state).

Maine

Maine has its own pluses and minuses. On the plus side, you can always find a remote and inexpensive property here. Which is an excellent option, since living off the grid is not living for free. Timber, rock and water are abundant and within a reach. The building codes are lenient, and an off-gridder is true welcomed.

On the other hand, the seasonal weather is not for everyone. The winter is cold and wet. However, the time from spring to fall is more tolerable and can be quite pleasant.

Missouri

The legality of living off the grid in the state of Missouri is unquestionable, and this life choice is even encouraged by the authorities! The state does not demand to connect to the septic systems or to have a well, and you can collect rainwater as you wish. Your choices are not heavily regulated by the local government, and the laws are in favor of those who wish to live a life independent of the rest of society.

The land in Missouri is very suitable for establishing a farm or a ranch, and nearby natural resources are abundant. When it comes to growing the crops, the weather is very helpful. While the summer tends to be too humid and sweltering for humans, it is actually useful for your livestock and farming intentions. Winter time, on the other hand, is mild with little snow, and some plants can still grow during the winter time. Add some rains around the year, and you get a climate that perfectly suits any off-the-grid desire.

There is an off-grid community in northeast Missouri known as Dancing Rabbit Ecovillage. 45 off-gridders in this community enjoy a simple style of life, while working on making a noticeable cultural change. The houses are built from recycled materials and run on renewable energy, making the ecovillage green and sustainable.

Montana

Montana can be a great choice if you intend to establish a ranch. But if you're buying a land there, you'd be better off in the mountains, which can shield you from the ruthless prairie winds. I would advise getting a mountain land in North Dakota and Wyoming as well. The Montana winter is cold, but it's more bearable in the mountains. You can also harness the power of the constant winds, and with the help of wind turbines turn it into a reliable power source.

Despite the weather, Montana is a place to be if you wish to live off the grid. The prices for the land are affordable, you can even find a property next to a water source for a good price. And again, if you go for the mountains and not the prairies, you can find a lot of rock and timber nearby.

The prairies and the grasslands are a great choice for livestock. Not so much for growing the plants, though, especially because of the shorter growing season. So consider raising a greenhouse to help your plants.

North Carolina

You can find a lot of superb and inexpensive land in North Carolina, just don't look near the coast line. NC has an ever-growing population of off-gridders, especially around the Black Mountain and the city of Saluda. If you wish to extend your preparedness and survival knowledge, the local Prepper Camp has everything you need.

A good example of what you can find in NC is Earthaven, a community based in the mountains near Asheville, North Carolina. It is a home to dozens of people, and the plans to extend this 320 acre community to 150 dwellers. The community's energy is supplied by hydropower and the sun.

Ohio

Ohio is often dismissed by those looking to settle off the grid, but it's actually a good option and has its well-earned place on this list. Let's have a separate list for Ohio's advantages (though mostly its southern half):

- Many natural resources
- Low land cost
- Affordable living costs
- Crime rates that are much lower than in most other states
- Property taxes are low as well
- No zoning regulations or permit office in many counties (the septic tank regulations, however, are managed by the health department)
- Long growing seasons for the crops, extending from May all the way to October

As you can see, Ohio is a real possibility, too.

Oregon

While some of Oregon is covered by the desert, you can find suitable lands in the Cascade Range Mountains and the entire western part of the state. Lots of natural resources, you can fish and hunt, as well as find quality timber on almost every lot.

The desert is not that bad either, it's high like in northern California, so the weather is easier to bear. And whatever part of Oregon you decide on, you can always find a land for an affordable price.

Three Rivers Recreation Area, situated in Central Oregon, is an impressive large off-the-grid community, housing over 600 residents. Three Rivers covers 4000 acres, and it's exclusively powered by solar panels. Thanks to the electricity produced from the sun, the local residents enjoy all the modern luxuries, such as satellite TV and fast Internet. There are also numerous ways to enjoy the outdoors, as you can go fishing, hunting, biking or even just relaxing under the clear skies. Whatever your budget is, you can always find there a property that suits you.

Another Oregon community is Breitenbush. Its 60-plus residents chose to go off the grid, and instead of relying on power lines, they use geothermal wells as a heat source. The community is quite open to visitors, its Hot Springs Retreat and Conference Center brings in tourists throughout the year. The visitors enjoy the stay in a unique community and the beautiful scenery.

Tennessee

Tennessee is the right place if you wish to save money (or even make money). It has it all. The taxes, the cost of living (in rural areas) and the property costs are the lowest in the United States. Natural resources, fishing and hunting, unsupervised rainwater collecting, 260 yearly days of growing season – the climate and the environment are on your side. All these attributes together make Tennessee one of the best off the grid possibilities.

Texas

Texas boasts countless acres of land that you can purchase. The land prices are really low in small counties and remote areas. Fishing and hunting are plentiful. However, water is a major problem, and the temperatures can get uncomfortably hot. After all, a significant part of Texas is a desert. This should not deter you from getting a nice deal that's easy on your pocket.

Vermont

Vermont is another recommended place for the off-grid life. First of all, the land prices are reasonable, and there is definitely a lot of land available. The natural resources, such as timber, rock and water, are also within a reach. Most counties have zoning laws that favor the off-grid residents, just choose a location far from the big towns.

Washington

Washington State is an excellent choice for those of us who dream of going off the grid in a green, luxuriant forest. The weather is moderate (45F in winter and 80F in summer), which makes Washington even more attractive.

While it does sound like a paradise, keep in mind that some local laws are extremely strict. They dictate just how you're allowed to build your house. But on the other hand, the laws also allow collecting rainwater and encourage raising various kinds of livestock. A lot of off-the-grid communities have already made Washington their permanent home. Furthermore, you can even purchase a lot that already has a ready-to-use off-the-grid property.

7 Factors to Consider Before Deciding Where to Live off the Grid in the USA

1. **Water source**. Going off the grid means disconnecting from the water lines. It would be better for you to buy a land near a steady and clean water source. This could be a lake, a river, a spring, or even a place with a functioning well. You cannot survive without water.
2. **Weather/climate**. Some people love the changing seasons, some would prefer a nice weather 365 days a year. Figure out what climate suits you the most, what

challenges you might be facing in the cold winter, in the hot summer, when it rains and when a tornado passes by. You can use a website like usa.com for a research, just look under "Historical Weather" for the area that interests you. And if the area is frequented by natural disasters (floods, earthquakes, drought, hurricanes, wildfires, and so on), then perhaps it's not worth the trouble. The number of sunny days per year can also affect whether you should go for off grid or on grid solar (click to learn the difference).

3. **Land cost**. This is not just about finding a price that fits your budget. A price tag for the land can hint about its quality. The land that's too cheap could mostly be a swamp or a desert. You probably should go for a land with natural resources and an agricultural quality. You could also consider buying a smaller lot and invest more money into the structure and equipment.
4. **Living costs**. Even if you plan to produce your own food and materials, there will always be something that you need to buy from a nearby shopping center. You could be spending quite a lot on the equipment before you see your first vegetables sprout. So research the cost of living in the state of your choosing and figure out if you can afford it.
5. **Local community**. It's also good to settle in an area populated with reliable and like-minded neighbors. These could be your newest friends. They can help you with their knowledge and information about the area, they will barter services and goods with you. Additionally, you probably wouldn't want a high population density nearby, should something extreme happen. Also, see what the crime rates are in this place. Low rates mean an easier protection of your land.
6. **Laws and regulations**. Nice weather and nice people can't improve your off-grid life should the local laws

be too limiting. Before moving to a state, ensure that you can achieve everything you planned. Do the local laws allow building a house that's not connected to the power grid? Are you penalized if your house is not linked to the sewage system? What are the building codes in this area? Do they demand that you use only certain materials when building a homestead? As you can see from these few examples, laws are not the same in every area, and they do not always fit the off-the-grid lifestyle.

7. **Property taxes**. These can take a huge chunk of your budget, so choose a state accordingly. Taxes can also affect your decision regarding the size of the land. A large land can be zoned as agricultural, therefore you will pay less taxes, but will need to pay upfront more when you purchase the land. On the other hand, a smaller (and cheaper) lot will be marked as a residential area, which means higher property taxes. See if you can **rezone a small property** as an agricultural zone by establishing a mini-farm (with or without livestock), or a garden.

ALASKA

Alaska deserves its own chapter. Not a lot of people are brave enough to live off the grid in Alaska, but there are those who have transferred their life to this remote state. Alaska is almost untouched by humans, making it peaceful, quiet and natural, allowing you to enjoy off grid living in the forest.

In this chapter, I will go through the important aspects of living off the grid in Alaska, and how you can plan and do it successfully.

Is It Legal to Live off the Grid in Alaska?

It is legal to live off the grid in Alaska, as long as you follow the rules of the state. In the USA, the laws and regulations differ from state to state, so it's not entirely legal to live off the grid in the USA wherever you please. When it comes to Alaska, it is legal, but it's always advised to check the laws of the state. This way you will avoid getting fined or prohibited from living off the grid wherever you wish. You should also become familiar with the local regulations regarding the production of solar and wind energy.

Generally speaking, as long as you're paying property and other taxes, the government should leave you alone. You must follow local building codes and zoning restrictions. Also, check local laws regarding rainwater collection, some places do not allow it.

For more information, refer to the previous chapter about the legality of living off the grid in the USA.

How Much Does It Cost to Live Off the Grid in Alaska?

The cost of living off the grid in Alaska can range from $80,000 to $300,000. Sure, it's not cheap but you must remember that you're changing the way you live entirely, and at first, you may need to spend and invest in your future living. With time, living off the grid will be less expensive than modern-urban living.

With that said, the cost varies depending if you prefer to build your own cabin or purchase a cabin that is already built, and also where in Alaska you're planning to live off the grid. A small cabin in an area that is less desirable can cost around $80,000, while a big cabin in a more primary location in Alaska can cost around $300,000.

Here are a few examples when discussing cost of off grid living in Alaska:

- **Small cabin (Seward, Alaska)**: a small cabin with 1 bedroom that is 0.52 acres in Seward can cost around $99,500.
- **Medium cabin (Willow, Alaska)**: a medium cabin with 3 bedrooms and 1.5 bathrooms that is 40 acres in Willow can cost around $190,000.
- **Large cabin (Trapper Creek, Alaska)**: a large cabin with 3 bedrooms and 1 bathroom that is 200 acres in Trapper Creek can cost around $385,000.

Bear in mind that this is not the entire amount you'll need to pay when considering starting life off the grid. There are other expanses to take in mind, like installing solar panels in order to generate power and energy (unless the cabin is already fully-equipped), getting equipment to raise livestock or grow fruits and vegetables (unless you're planning to purchase food in a store), and more.

Again, the cost varies according to your needs and plans. Some prefer to live entirely off the grid and grow their own food in solitude, while other prefer to live away from the city and the urban life, but still purchase at the store and enjoy modern technologies and appliances.

Alaska off Grid Living: Things to Consider

In order to make a successful transition to living off the grid in Alaska, there are a few crucial things to consider, including location, terrain, sunlight, access, water, temperature, and others.

- **Location**: First, you have to decide how far away and secluded your cabin to be. Some people prefer to live far away as possible, while others prefer to live off the grid, but still close enough to a nearby town for shopping, groceries, supplies, or even enjoy a day trip from time to time.
- **Permits and zoning**: Always check for permits and what the law states when considering buying a piece of land or building a property. You can't just start building wherever you please, and there are specific rules and regulations what you are allowed to build and what not on the land you own. For example, there may be areas where you are allowed to build only a one story home, or live near a lake, yet you are prohibited from using it as a source of water. So, as I stated earlier, always check the law, rules, permits and regulations.
- **Taxation**: This is actually not a problem when considering off grid living in Alaska. Just wanted to mention here and let you know that when it comes to taxation in Alaska, it is the lowest in USA. Alaska does not have income tax, sales tax, estate tax and inheritance tax. There are only 25 municipalities that demand taxation when it comes to property.
- **Terrain**: This is also an important factor to consider. Alaska is a vast place, and it's not all trees. Even be-

tween the forests, there are spaces that are wide open. Also, the soil is not the same in different areas in Alaska, so consider it as well. If you want to grow your own food, make sure that the soil is suitable for it, and that there is enough sunlight in the area.

- **Access**: You need to consider access points and routes to your off grid home. Consider how you will be going off and getting to the house. Will you be using a car / SUV / boat / small plane (not uncommon at all in Alaska, depending on the terrain)? If the land you're purchasing to build your cabin is already developed, then there will probably be established roads there as well. However, this isn't always the case. If the road is not 100% suitable for a car, you should get an SUV. Also, consider getting sleds or even a snowmobile for the winter and cold months. After all, it is Alaska we're talking about.
- **Sunlight**: Sunlight is important to grow food and support a garden, trees and plants, but also to generate energy using solar panels, which is the most common and popular way to generate power while living off the grid. So, if you're planning to generate power using solar panels, make sure that there is enough sunlight in the area. Additionally, get several batteries to store enough energy for the sunless days.
- **Water**: There are many fresh springs and lakes in Alaska, which comes in your favor. It is best to have access to these sources of water, but also make sure to have the necessary rights and permits to use this water. Of course, you shouldn't use the water straight from the lake, and must purify and distill it for safe usage and consumption. Another way to have and use water is by collecting rainwater. You can easily construct a rainwater catchment. If access to water is unavailable, your best option will be to drill a well

on the land you've purchased. Again, it's important to know all rules, restrictions and get the desired permits before you start any kind of drilling.

- **Temperature and weather:** Alaska is big, and the weather can differ from one area to another. The more you go north, the colder it will get, so it's important to know how much cold you're willing to endure. There are even locations in Alaska where temperature can get as low as 40-60 degrees Fahrenheit below zero. Also, during the winter, it is very cold in interior areas as well as in The Arctic. As for the average annual snowfall, we are talking about 74 inches, as well as 16.57 inches for precipitation. Be prepared for low and cold temperatures and be safe during the winter.
- **Homeschooling**: If you plan to move to Alaska with your family and have children, you should know that there are no laws in Alaska for homeschooling. This means that you do not have to notify authorities or anyone else if you prefer to teach your kids alone at home, and no one will check or inspect this issue.
- **Farm animals and gardening**: Alaska is very easy going with its laws, and if you're planning to raise farm animals and occupy yourself with gardening, here is what you should know: there are no restrictions or any prohibition when it comes to gardening. As for farm animals, you can raise them only if you are able to provide them with warm housing and fenced pastures.

Once you considered all these factors, the off grid living in Alaska can be quite possible.

Useful Tips

Now that you have an idea about what it is like living off the grid in Alaska, I would like to share some tips that may be useful when preparing and moving to Alaska.

1. **Getting used to being alone**: Living off the grid in a remote location is nothing like living in the city surrounded by friends, family and other people. Yes, you will enjoy peace and quiet, no one to bother you or suffer from noise, but for some people this can get crazy after a while. That is why it is crucial that you learn to live peacefully with yourself and alone. There are ways to learn being okay while living alone. You can learn to meditate, do yoga, read books, write letters, move with a family or a friend, occupy yourself or have a pet living with you. If there are any neighbors around or close to you, get to know them and enjoy some company and new friends. If the area you're based at has satellite or cell service, you can make some calls and talk to friends and family from time to time as well.
2. **Accept and respect nature**: Remember that you're living now in the territory of wild animals. It is important to be careful and thread lightly. Always be safe, never try to engage if you're not in any danger, and respect the animals and their surroundings. Alaska is home to many animals, among them are bears, moose, deer and other creatures. If you don't interfere in their way and they don't feel alarmed, scared or in danger, they won't come your way and will leave you alone as well. Respect the boundaries and consider building a fence around the area of the garden. However, bear in mind (pun intended) that some animals may at times climb over the fence and enjoy the fruits of your labor. So, don't try to fight big animals that can injure or even kill you. Instead, best to plant more and be prepared to share.
3. **Learn how to shop for groceries and supplies**: When living off the grid in a remote and secluded area, shopping needs to be adjusted as well. You're not in the

city anymore, so you won't just drop by at the store if you ran out of milk or the kids want a snack all of a sudden. Depending how far away you live from the nearest town or grocery shop, you'll have to buy supplies and food that will last for weeks or even months. Buy products that last for a long period of time, get flour, canned foods, butter, sugar, water, and anything you need that can last and is non-perishable until your next purchase.

4. **Grow your own food**: You can always grow your own food, which will save you a lot of money as well as hustle to get to the store. There's also a great sense of accomplishment and pride in consuming something you've grown all by yourself, and it will probably even taste better. Of course the area, soil, amount of water, sunlight and everything else needed to grow your own food needs to be suitable. It is advised to grow food during the summer in order to preserve it for the months of winter. You can build a greenhouse or invest in one. This will allow you to prolong the growing season and not rely only on summertime, as well as growing food that can be difficult or even impossible in Alaska.
5. **Getting used to the dark**: At some areas of Alaska, like the northern corners of the state, it is very dark for months. Even in interior areas of Alaska it gets pretty dark during the winter, as daylight becomes shorter. It's not easy to live in the dark and can bring on depression, but it's a part of living in Alaska, getting used to the dark and not having it affect your mood.
6. **Hobbies**: I've already mentioned that it can be quite challenging at the wilderness, secluded, away from anything and anyone and during the winter when you'll be spending most of your time at the cabin, it's important to find something to keep you busy and

occupied. A hobby is good for the mind, the soul and even the body. If your hobby requires supplies, get as much as needed for months ahead. It can be anything you love doing and is available where you're at. Painting, sculpting, knitting, anything you desire that makes you busy and happy. On your next shopping trip to town, purchase all the required supplies and even get some extra in case something gets lost, ruined or broken. You can also read books, watch movies, so whatever your preferred activity is, it is important to keep yourself occupied and entertained.

7. **Exercise:** It is crucial that you keep yourself strong and healthy, especially when the nearest town and medical services are far away. Plan a weekly routine and keep at it. You will feel better (emotionally, mentally and physically), become stronger and healthier. An exercise is great for the body, but also for your mind. And, being in Alaska, you can always add wood chopping to your plan, in case you need to burn wood to keep you warm at nights and during winter.
8. **Outhouse/composting toilet**: Not all cabins off the grid include a toilet, so one solution is using an outhouse as a toilet. Septic systems are not always available when living off the grid so far away. Many people who live off the grid in Alaska use outhouses, so it's very common there. How and where to place the outhouse is all up to you. Some prefer to place them farther from the cabin or house in order to be safe from the smell that may arise. Another great option is a composting toilet. They are convenient, used indoors and there is almost no smell at all coming out of them. It's also a great option during the winter when you simply want to stay inside the house, for all purposes.
9. **Wood stacking**: One way to heat the house and keep yourself warm is using heat from wood. You can al-

ways check for installation of solar panels and use the sun as your source of energy, but if you wish to save money and prefer old-school living, wood is the way to go. Wood chipping can take the entire summer, but you're preparing for the cold and dark winter. Split the wood in two using an axe and then pile it all orderly together. Having someone to do this work for you may be quite expensive. The location of your living will determine how cold it gets during winter and how much wood you will burn. This can be between 5 to 15 cords of wood during a single winter. Another way to heat the house is using oil. The downside is that it also can get expensive and you can't afford to run out of it, especially during winter when it's freezing and the roads may be blocked, not allowing you to get into town to re-new the supply.

10. **Communication/Internet**: Living off the grid and secluded far away in Alaska can be a dream come true, but it's smart to have a way to communicate with the "outside world", especially at times of trouble and during emergencies. There are places where there is no cell signal or satellite communication, so it's best to have a way that will allow you to stay connected. There are off grid communication devices that do not require cell service or Wi-Fi for them to work (goTenna Mesh, Garmin inReach Explorer+), and there is a way to get off grid Internet as well.
11. **Get a seasonal job**: Living off the grid in Alaska is not always cheap. Sometimes, materials and equipment that are usually cheap in other states can be more expensive in Alaska. If you need money or don't want to get stranded without it, you can get a seasonal job and earn some cash. It's pretty easy to find a seasonal job in Alaska, thanks to their thriving tourism industry that lasts for 5 months. That leaves you the rest of the year

to relax and enjoy your off grid living in Alaska.

CANADA: IS IT LEGAL?

Recent years saw a steep rise in people desiring to live off grid in Canada. Consequently, there are a lot of questions and debates whether this is legal or not. As a proponent of the off grid living, I did some research to give a clear and concrete answer.

Is It Illegal to Live Off Grid in Canada?

As you understand by now, "off grid" means that your abode is not connected to the country's power grid. The off-gridders produce their own electricity, usually by using solar panels. They also tend to cultivate a garden, growing their own crops or even livestock. This arrangement can work as a **self-sustained miniature farm**. And it's perfectly legal.

However, some restrictions apply. There is a somewhat known case in the off grid community, about a woman in Nova Scotia. She tried to live in her own tiny off-grid house, because she did not wish to leave a footprint on the world. A commendable, ecologically aware desire. But then the local authority has denied her occupancy. **The building codes** demand that every occupied space must have ventilation and smoke detectors.

Her house now stands empty, because there are restrictions that you must be mindful of. Always check your local building codes. In her case, **a solution actually exists**. She can install smoke detectors and a ventilation system, and power them by batteries or a solar collector.

Can I Live Off Grid if I Don't Own The Land?

Here is where the real troubles start. There are no squatter rights in Canada. You can't just place your small house or tent on a random patch of land. **The law will come after you.** It's even worse if you are not an actual Canadian resident.

There is also a question of how "off grid" you desire to be. The aforementioned Nova Scotian lady was somewhat extreme, as she intended to live without the electricity. Some imagine "off grid" as **completely living in the woods**, hunting and foraging. But how many of us truly wish to give up on all the benefits of the modern civilization?

This is where **the land ownership** once again comes into play. Building on someone else's lot prevents you from enjoying some of the common comforts. For instance, receiving letters and parcels with your online purchases. The Canadian government and Canada Post will not play along with your off grid initiative. They already have their own system of street names and house numbers. The governing body will not accept any illegal subdivision of the land that already has a permanent address.

The same goes for other services you'd like to have in your off grid home. Purists might scoff at this, but some of us would still like to enjoy an access to the Internet, a phone, maybe a satellite TV. These, of course, are supplied by various companies, and the companies will require **a legal street address** before they install their services.

Do You Have to Pay Taxes If You Live off the Grid?

Living off the grid usually does not mean you become a completely free man, who stands up to the government and is completely independent of the country's laws. You can grow your own food and produce your own electricity, but **it is not possible to completely avoid taxes**.

First of all, there are the usual **income taxes** that every citizen pays. Even if you see yourself ideologically free from the state and the government, no one can avoid the taxman forever. You might be self-sufficient, but the state still need the money to fix the roads, among other things.

Additionally, even if you have the permit to build and you own the property, there are of course **property taxes**. These mostly depend on the square footage, but also on several other factors, such as the geographical location. Find out what the local law in your area says about the property taxes before you decide the settle.

Can I Insure Myself If I'm Living off the Grid?

The off-gridders invest a lot of time and sometimes money into their homes. So, along with the legality question, they started asking whether they can be covered by insurance. The solar panels alone can sometimes cost tens of thousands of dollars, a solid investment that should be insured. Not to mention the house, its surroundings and, of course, the people living there.

This is where it gets tricky, according to many insurance companies. Among their concerns is the off grid lifestyle. If you live with no heat or water, **they will refuse to insure you**. If your house has a stove or a fireplace and is made of wood, they will see it as a fire hazard and, again, will refuse to insure. What you should do is to consult with a representative of a more willing company and see whether you need to upgrade your house in order to get it insured. If you have taken all the necessary precautions, if you are not living in unhealthy conditions, then **the insurance is possible**.

All in all, different provinces have different laws and living conditions, which is why I would like to invite you to read my chapter on the best places to live off the grid in Canada.

CANADA: BEST PLACES FOR OFF GRID LIVING

Canada, of course, is not a small country. Different areas and provinces provide us with different options for settlement and off the grid living. Access to water, soil type, climate, and so on – all these factors should be taken into account during the decision making process.

So where is the best place to live off the grid in Canada? The list of best off grid places in Canada includes:

- The Rocky Mountains in Alberta
- The Okanagan Valley and Western Rockies in British Columbia
- The south of New Brunswick
- Some parts of the Maritime Provinces

A longer answer to this question is not a simple one, since every place has its own advantages. It is up to you to choose which province or territory sounds the best. And it is up to me to give you the most focused and essential information there is. So let's check what off-the-grid Canada has to offer, shall we?

The Best Places to Live off the Grid in Canada

Alberta

The best off-the-grid area in Alberta is near the Canadian Rockies (the Canadian part of the North American Rocky Mountains). The foothills there have fertile soil, while the crops are protected by the mountains from the harsh, cold winds. Another good location is the area around Red Deer and Edmonton.

Not every spot in Alberta fits the off-the-grid lifestyle. Places like Banff & Lake Louise attract too much tourism, and the land there is far from being affordable. There are also military bases east to the Rockies, which you should avoid.

And then there are Canadian Prairies. While living on a grassland sounds like a possibility, the weather is far from inviting. During the winter, the cold air mass comes from the Arctic region. The temperatures get extremely low, preventing from building an off-the-grid farm and homestead.

In conclusion, while some of the regions of Alberta are highly desirable, others are best avoided.

British Columbia

Probably the best place to live off the grid in Canada is the Okanagan Valley, situated in British Columbia. This central piece of the province, located above the state of Washington, has it all:

- Great climate
- Fertile land
- Growing seasons
- Lakes
- Forests
- Small towns with helpful community
- Safety from earthquakes and tsunamis

As you can see, the Okanagan is a terrific place to start your off the grid life. Another nearby location is to the north of the valley, by the foothills of the Rockies. This location also has fertile soil and moderate weather, so you definitely should check it out.

Manitoba

The southern part of Manitoba is considered being more suitable for crops, with an abundance of lakes as a steady water source. The downside is the weather. Not only is there a danger of tornadoes, but the summers are extremely humid and warm. The uncomfortable climate might deter some of the off-gridders from choosing this area.

Maritime Provinces

I included Prince Edward, Nova Scotia and Newfoundland islands under this category, since their off-the-grid living conditions are very similar. These are large islands, yet the population density is low and tolerable. The Maritime islands are close to the mainland, which can be another plus.

The climate can be quite pleasant, without extreme ranges, thanks to the Atlantic Gulf Stream that calms the weather. The weather here is noticeably warmer, if you compare it to the western or central parts of the country, or even to the state of Maine to the south.

The land is very suitable for the crops, especially on Nova Scotia. The Maritime Island Provinces are also known for their moderate land prices. All in all, they sound like a good option to establish your homestead here.

New Brunswick

If you look at the eastern half of Canada, you will realize that the south of New Brunswick is the most welcoming region to those who wish to live off the grid. This area has it all:

- It's sparsely populated, so you don't have to worry about having too many people nearby.
- The land is most suitable for farming.
- Hilly ground leaves a lot of space to be dug under your

house, where you can store the produced food.

- The Atlantic Ocean is nearby, so you can add fish and seafood to your dining table.

It's almost an ideal place, but once again, you need to consider the weather. The summers here can get very humid and filled with bugs. The winters are wet and very chilly. If you can handle this kind of weather, then southern New Brunswick is the place to be.

Ontario

Similar to other territories and provinces, not all areas of Ontario are the best locations for off the grid living. For this province, however, the reason is that the region near the Great Lakes is heavily populated. There is no option to be far away from the power grids and the crowds.

But **there is still a good land for off-grid living in Ontario, mostly to the northwest of Peterborough**. You will be removed enough from the rest of the civilization, yet if you need supplies, they are just a short drive away.

It is possible to live for years in a tiny house in Northern Ontario, as this woman has proven:

Quebec

The options in Quebec are somewhat limited, but if you don't mind living in the hills and mountains, then there is enough land for you there. Just drive northwest about half an hour either from Montreal or Quebec City, and you're set.

Saskatchewan

Compared to Manitoba and some other provinces, Saskatchewan has less water sources available. On the other hand, about half of all Canadian grains grow in Saskatchewan, which means that this province is mainly plains.

This can be good news for those of us who do not wish to

live among the mountains. On the other hand, the temperature changes throughout the year are pretty radical. Saskatchewan holds the records for the highest and the lowest temperatures in Canada. These facts can deter some of the folks from choosing this region. If you insist on living here, find a forest with a spring or a small river nearby.

Rest of Canada

The opportunities to establish an off-grid homestead in northern parts of Canada are limited. Only the toughest survivalists will take upon themselves the challenge of living in a very cold climate and almost never-ending winter. We are talking about such parts of the country as Nunavut, Yukon, Northwest Territories, Newfoundland and Labrador.

The same goes for the northern halves of the aforementioned provinces: Alberta, British Columbia, Manitoba, Saskatchewan and Quebec. Anything mentioned under "Rest of Canada" is not among the best off-the-grid areas. I simply list them to cover the entire map. If you wish to start a new life, living in a removed, isolated, barren place will not keep your spirits up. Better start in the places I recommended earlier.

The Off-the-Grid Communities of Canada

You can establish your own homestead on a remote lot, away from other people – or you can join one of the existing off-the-grid communities in Canada. Places like Yellowknife, NT have well-known communities that live off-grid and enjoy the freedom of their life choices. Yellowknife offers a great experience for people from all walks of life. **You don't even have to build a house – you can rent one for almost nothing.**

Then there is the **Lasqueti island**, not far from Vancouver. Its community of 400 people grow their own corn and forage for food. The power comes from the solar panels and wind turbines. The houses are built from recycled or natural materials, and look very adorable, if I may say so.

On the other side of Vancouver, in Cypress Bay near the town of Tofino, is the **Freedom Cove**. This unique and small off-grid community actually floats on the water, as it's built from 12 floating platforms. The couple that built it have created a guest house, art studio, greenhouses, even a dance floor! The greenhouses and the fishing provide this off-grid family with enough food around the year, since they don't own a refrigerator.

UNITED KINGDOM

Is it possible to live off the grid in the UK? The short answer is yes. You can live off the grid in the UK and start experiencing a free and independent life. More than that, living off the grid also means you save a lot of money in the long run. The environment will supply you with energy, heat, water and food.

Of course, there are challenges along the way. The transformation to this new life can be difficult and may even seem impossible. However, many people around the world did it, and they fully embraced this off the grid lifestyle, despite the difficulties. So here is how it can be done in the UK as well.

Starting Your off Grid Living in the UK: Step by Step

Finding and Choosing a Location

This is probably the first and most important thing when planning to live off the grid. You need to find land that is both affordable and suitable for off grid living. If you live in the UK, consider buying a piece of land for your new house. However, don't forget to check if you still need to pay council tax that correlates to the size of your purchased lot. Check the local laws to avoid accidentally breaking them.

Once you find a suitable land, you will probably need to learn and follow local planning restrictions before you can start building your new off grid home (see below).

Here are a few more important things to consider when deciding on a type of a land:

- **Woodland**: A very good option, since wood can be a

fuel source as well as a building material.

- **Arable land**: A fertile land that allows you to grow food on your own as well as raise livestock.
- **Water source**: You can choose a location that is near a water source, as there is no life without water. Fresh water is crucial for survival, so prefer a location near a stream, river or well, and remember to purify the water if needed.

Planning Permission

If you plan to live the off grid lifestyle in a static caravan or a yurt, then you don't have to worry about planning permission. But, if you're planning to live in a permanent home, then you would need go through the UK Planning Permission System.

You will need planning permission in the following cases:

- When you are planning to build something new
- When you want to make a big change to your building
- When you want to change the use of the building

For more about UK planning permission and to learn how to apply for it, you can visit the Planning Permission website.

Power Source

Living off the grid does not mean you have to live in the dark, like in the old days. You can still generate power and enjoy modern appliances. You can charge your laptop or cellphone, you can use TV, portable oven, washing machine, and other devices that make your living more convenient.

The most popular choice to generate power when living off the grid is by installing solar panels on the roof of your new home. Bear in mind that you will need batteries to store this energy. Also, each appliance uses different amount of energy, so see that you have enough batteries to store all the electricity that your homestead requires.

Some homesteads use wind (wind turbines). Others use water power (hydroelectric power) to generate electricity, if they are close to a water source, although the setup can be pretty expensive. Like I said before, the most common source to generate power and electricity is by using solar panels.

Water

If you can live near a water source, which can supply water for drinking, cooking, washing and basically living, that would be great. However, that is not always possible. So, your options for water sources can come from rainwater and bore water. Naturally, you should purify and sterilize the water before consumption because it can be contaminated.

Collecting rainwater is always a possibility, but you will probably need an underground water tank to collect the water and then filter it using a special system. This setup can cost £10,000 or more.

As for a borehole, you will require a geological survey. Fortunately, there are services and companies in the UK that arrange such a survey and even drill the borehole for you.

Another interesting option is using something that is called Off Grid Box. It can provide you with drinking water as well as electricity almost anywhere in the world. This box is mostly used in developing countries, or those who choose to live off the grid. It can be deployed even in case of a natural disaster. For more information, see part 3, chapter "Contracting and Consultation".

Heating

Heat pumps are probably the best option, efficiency-wise, when it comes to heating your off-grid house. This incredible invention operates by taking the underground heat. Alternatively, they can take the heat from the outside, bringing warm air into the house.

Other options to heat your home are through **biomass** (which means burning wood or using organic matter) and **thermal collectors**. You can also purchase portable heating appliances and products that are not bad at all for heating purposes.

Food

If you truly want to live and feed off the grid, then it's time for you to grow your own food. You can grow vegetables, fruits, grains, raise livestock for the purposes of dairy products and meat, build a coop, and more. I got into greater detail on this subject in part 3, chapter "Farming".

Drainage and Waste Disposal

Sometimes, this subject is neglected and overlooked, yet you must have a plan for disposal of waste. An improper disposal not only damages the land, nature and environment, but can also lead to fines.

There are two common and popular ways to dispose of waste:

- **Composting toilet**: Many off-gridders install composting toilets. They are waterless, compact in their size, and do not smell (completely odorless).
- **Soakaway**: This is a simple hole that you dig in the ground. It is filled with coarse stone and rubble, which allows the surface water to percolate back into the ground. The hole should be 1 meter deep (give or take).

5 Amazing Places in UK to Experience the off Grid Living

Starting an off grid lifestyle is a big challenge that for sure can be life changing. So, before you disconnect yourself from the city and urban city-life, here are 5 amazing places in UK where you can get a glimpse what off the grid living is all about.

- **Guardswell Farm, Perthshire**: The guests in this beautiful place are asked to turn off everything and switch off entirely. This means no Wi-Fi, you just soak the breathtaking views. The farm is located on a hilltop between the small villages of Kinnaird and Abernyte. There are self-catering options, sleeping cabins for two, or a farmhouse for 10. Lights are available thanks to solar power, but there is no fridge. For your cooking, you get to choose between a woodburner, gas hob and outdoor fire pit. There's a foldout sofa bed available for children. **Cost**: From £130 a night.

- **Laggan, Ardnish Peninsula**: This is a whitewashed cottage on a private land that is 3,500 acres. You can access it only by sea, and there is no electricity. Feel free to enjoy a cozy and romantic feeling from the woodburners and paraffin lamps. You are close to the water edge with a stunning view. There is also wildlife that include red deer, white-tailed eagles and seals. In order to get to the nearest neighborhood, you'd have to walk for 3 hours or take a 10-minute trip by boat. There are playing cards and games, but you will be surrounded 100% by nature and its sounds. **Cost**: £900 a week. Sleeping is up to five in two bedrooms and a cabin.
- **Old Coach House, near Looe on the south coast, Cornwall**: Narrow tracks as well as winding lanes lead you to Old Coach House, which is an amazing Victorian property. It consists of three bedrooms in a 70 acres of private land. There are also fields and wild gardens for your pleasure, and even a path (although steep) that takes you down to the private beach. Here, you experience what off grid living is all about. You get electricity for the fridge and the lights from solar panels, and you cook using a gas hob or a woodburner. There are no neighbors nearby, and the world feels far, far away. There are many games and books, a guitar and even African drums. Don't worry, there's also a homebuilt,

wood-fired hot tub. **Cost**: From £89 a night, up to eight people.

- **Chartners Farm, Northumberland**: Located 20 miles from the Scottish boarder, this is a new off-the-grid bunkhouse for up to 12 people. Solar panels and wind turbines generate electricity, and a huge logburner makes sure the place is warm. However, there is no Wi-Fi. Instead, you can take a walk through the beautiful woods and cycle along the Sandstone Way, which is a new route for biking. You can enjoy a barbecue place as well as a terrace, which are ideal in the summer. You can even camp in the surroundings with tents and sleeping bags. Also, you can arrange to take the dog with you. **Cost**: £95 a night (two-night minimum), up to 12 people in three rooms.
- **Shank Wood Log Cabin, Cumbria:** This stunning wood log cabin is located on a river bank and is surrounded by woodland. It was built from local timber. This is where you truly get the feeling of off grid living by going back to nature. In here, all you will hear is running water as there is no cellphone signal, no Wi-Fi, no TV and no fridge. There's a wood-fired hut tub, and the lights are provided using solar panels. Basically, this place is all about getting in touch with nature and the environment. This place is perfect for a family, as it includes two double beds, kitchen, living area and a woodburning stove. **Cost**: From £150 a night, up to four people, and a minimum of two nights.

AUSTRALIA

Off the grid living is becoming more and more popular in Australia, as many families decide to leave society and start enjoying the freedom of living off the grid. Similarly to other countries, when you live off the grid in Australia, you provide your own power source, water supply, food, and so on. You don't rely on any other source but your own skills and produce.

So what should you know before living off the grid in Australia? There are several important factors to consider:

- Is it legal to live off the grid in Australia?
- What permits are needed?
- What skills and knowledge are needed?
- How do I provide power, water and food?
- Are there off grid communities in Australia?

In this chapter, I will answer these and other important questions regarding living off the grid in Australia. First, let us take a look why this lifestyle is on the rise in Australia.

Why is Off the Grid Living Becoming so Popular in Australia?

Housing costs in Australia continue to rise. Because of that, more and more people in Australia consider living off the grid. Standalone power systems as well as the eco-friendly lifestyle have quickly become an attractive and realistic option.

The goal of off-grid homes is to achieve autonomy instead of relying on a city's water, gas, electricity and sewerage. Such lifestyle allows you to live more responsibly and be more sustainable.

In the past 10 years, more and more people have chosen to start living off the grid, especially due to the long-run advantages. Sure, there are initial costs to spend as you prepare everything needed to live off the grid. But, once you've settled in, the returns are big. Eventually, you will see the financial, emotional and health benefits of this life-changing decision.

People who are already living off the grid have stated that once you start living this way, it can pay for itself within 3 to 5 years.

Besides the rising costs of urban living, people in Australia decide to live off the grid for the following reasons:

- It gives them the option to control their own utilities.
- They can grow their own food and have many choices which are much healthier than the mass-produced food.
- They disconnect themselves from the stress and pressures of everyday urban living.
- It allows them to enjoy a healthier and calmer lifestyle.

Is It Legal to Live Off the Grid in Australia?

The answer is that **it isn't illegal to live off the grid in Australia**. However, it comes with some conditions and limitations:

- **Permits regarding zoning and housing**: Every county and town have different laws when it comes to off grid living. Therefore, you should check off grid living regulations in the specific zone and area you're interested in.
- **Incentives and rebates**: The Australian government may reward you with different incentives once you start your off grid living. These incentives can help you offset the costs of starting this kind of lifestyle.

- **Ownership and land**: You may need to find special land for sale, if you want to build an off-the-grid house on it.

Therefore, before planning and starting to build, always check the laws that govern construction and use of land in order not to break any local laws.

How to Know if Off the Grid Living in Australia is for You

There's a big difference between thinking and planning to start living off the grid, and actually taking actions and start living that way.

In order to really know if off the grid living in Australia is for you, see how you answer the following checklist:

- Can you live without the comfort you got used to in the modern society?
- Are you willing to learn to repair on your own?
- Are you self-sufficient, creative and can handle challenging situations and circumstances?
- Are you willing to work hard, and even get dirty if necessary?

If none of the things in this checklist scare you, then you may have what it takes to start living off the grid in Australia.

Factors to Consider When Deciding to Live Off the Grid in Australia

1. Finding Land

If you don't own any land and don't have a home that you would like to convert to off the grid living, then you need to start looking for a place and a home. Don't worry, this does not mean you'll have to look for a place at the Outback.

2. Getting Permits

Australian people who decided to go and live off the grid haven't cut themselves entirely from society. They simply chose to live their lives from now on without the worries and expanses of typical urban living.

In order to start living off the grid, you may need to get planning and council permits that approve the construction of your new home.

There are off the grid experts that suggest you secure a land that does not require getting permits to build or live on. However, this option isn't always practical when it comes to you and your family. The areas that do not require permits are often remote areas, meaning they are far away from towns, schools and other people.

Basically, the farther your land is, chances are slim that you'll require permits for off the grid living in that remote area.

3. Getting Power and Food

When you live off the grid, you provide the power, food and water for your homestead. This means growing your own food, heating and cooling your home on your own, removing waste, providing electricity through independent power sources, and more.

Producing your own electricity can be achieved by installing solar panels or by using generators and batteries. If you are afraid about the cost, there is no need to be. As technology keeps improving, the cost of solar implementation continues to decrease.

Another great option for power source is using wind energy. This is most useful if you are based far away from the cities and in open locations. Wind energy can produce a lot of power very fast. You can even store excess power. Storing power is possible, since the off grid setups usually come with another battery or two that store the power for future use.

Living off the grid does not mean you can't enjoy electronics and up-to-date appliances such as working with a laptop, charging your cell phone, or even using a washing machine. It simply means that you will need to have enough power and energy to run them.

Producing your own water can be achieved by building a well or living near a water source. If you draw water from a natural stream or lake, remember that the water needs to be purified before you use it.

Before you begin living off the grid, see that you can provide all this for yourself and not be dependent on society or a nearby city.

Off the Grid Communities in Australia

In Australia, there are various communities for people who chose to live off the grid. Here are a few examples of such communities:

- **Chewton Bushlands**: In 1967, two people bought a block of land located in Victorian bushlands. The two had dreamt to live an alternative lifestyle, and 50 years later, there are 35 households living the off the grid dream.
- **Cohousing Australia Initiative**: They promote collective models of housing, housing choices and diversity. Cohousing is a unique way of establishing an off the grid community, I invite you to visit their website for additional info.
- **Tiny Homes Foundation Australia**: This non-profit organization strives to provide housing solutions that are highly affordable and sustainable. This Australian initiative is fully dedicated to promote housing which is environmentally, socially and economically viable.

BEST PLACES IN THE WORLD TO LIVE OFF THE GRID

As you understand by now, off the grid living allows you to fully connect to beautiful nature and Mother Earth. Live a life free of stress, save a lot of money, be independent of urban infrastructures – this is what off the gird living is all about. You can have a healthier life as you grow your own food and use nature's resources if you choose to.

Still, starting an off grid living is a huge life-changing decision. In fact, it's one of the biggest decisions you will ever face. However, only a few people know where to live this lifestyle and where are the best places to live off the grid.

In this chapter, I will share with you some of the best places to live off the grid in the world, so no matter where you are from, your next off grid home may be very close to you. A few of them are more suitable for a visit or vacation only, but they also a part of off the grid experience. But first, let us look at the relevant factors that affect your decision.

Factors to Consider When Choosing an Off the Grid Location

Not every place and location is good for off the grid living. You need to be selective and choose a place that suits your and your family's needs. Here are the top factors to consider when looking for an off grid location:

- **Pollution**: You would want to choose a location that is free of pollution. This means avoiding living next to drilling operations, mining operations, factories, power plants, waste and garbage disposal facilities, and even large farms. It is recommended to live at least 200 miles away from any of these buildings and operations.
- **Access to water**: First of all, you can't live without water, and second, there is no way to be self-sufficient without access to water. Therefore, your off the grid location must have access to clean water. Look for a place near a river, stream, lake or underground water source. It is also recommended to look for a place that receives at least some rain during the year for clean water and for living things around to grow. If necessary, **purify the water** to be 100% sure that it is clean. Digging your own well is also an option, but not every lot has available groundwater.
- **Access to roads**: Living off the grid doesn't mean you have to entirely disconnect yourself from the world. You actually want to have access to roads, especially if an emergency arises. Access to roads also have influences on the property's price and cost. If the property has access to roads, its cost will be higher. Access to maintained public roads is crucial in a case of an emergency or in case you need to evacuate your property.
- **Regulations**: Try looking for an off grid location with minimal regulations and zoning laws. The reason is less bureaucracy and permits to live off the grid in that location. You will also pay less money to local government and the state.
- **Coastal areas**: It is not recommended to live near coastal areas, as they can suffer from earthquakes (especially on the U.S. West Coast), hurricanes, and even military invasion. Try choosing a place that is more

inland and avoid living near coastal areas.

Now that you know what to check and look for when choosing an off the grid location, let's have a look at some of the best places and locations for off the grid living (or just for an off the grid trip and vacation).

Top 20 Places in the World to Live off the Grid

Dancing Rabbit Ecovillage, Missouri (USA)

Before deciding whether this place is good for you to start your off grid living, you should first visit it. Dancing Rabbit Ecovillage allows people to visit the place, and they use renewable energy in order to sustain their way of living.

Because this community has become somewhat of an expert in the use of wind and solar power, they even export some of that energy. The village started developing back in 1997. A group of people decided to buy the land where the town is currently located.

People who visit the place and want to get a glimpse and understand the way of life there have several options and programs to choose from. This community can be a great place for people looking to live off the grid and start enjoying a lifestyle that is fully independent.

Greater World Earthship Community, Taos, New Mexico (USA)

The people in this community live in exclusive and unique homes that are energy efficient. These homes are known as "Earthship", and they use solar as well as wind power in order to run them.

Michael Reynolds, an architect, was the one who suggested the idea and designed these special homes using only recycled and natural materials. In order to produce energy, people in this community collect water as well as maintain snow reservoirs. Then they treat the water and reuse it time and time again.

This off the grid community has grown and developed into an amazing place to live in, and today it even manufactures biodiesel fuel.

Three Rivers Recreation Area, Oregon (USA)

This place actually started out as a vacation place for people to get some rest and relax from daily stress and modern life. It seems that some of the people fell in love with the place, as they decided to stay there and build a community for those who are interested in off the grid living.

The location of the place is in Central Oregon, and it consists of small residential homes as well as large vacation homes.

Today, more than 600 people live in the area and produce energy using solar and wind power for their everyday living. This place is perfect for those who wish to live the off grid lifestyle, yet still want to enjoy aspects of modern day living.

Lasqueti Island, British Columbia (Canada)

This is without a doubt one of the most beautiful places in the world and perhaps your next location for off the grid living. Many nature lovers constantly visit this place, as well as people who want to start a new life, away from modern urban living and begin an off the grid lifestyle.

To this day, approximately 400 people live there without any connection to British Columbia power systems, meaning all 400 live the off grid lifestyle and are doing so happily.

The place is filled with trees that are 1,000 years old and because of it, is perfect and ideal for those who look to feel and be part of nature, living a quieter and healthier life. Apart from it being stunningly beautiful, this place is very peaceful and quiet. If you love nature, this is the perfect place for you.

Torri Superiore (Italy)

This place is actually an ecovillage that mixes eco-friendly and medieval Italian ways of life. This solar-powered community is guided by eco-friendly principles, and these principles helped them to be the prosperous community that they are today.

The community warmly welcomes people who wish to learn about their off the grid lifestyle. They even invite the people and guests into the village to have a look at their lives. This small village is home to 20 residents who are permanent there, but they also gladly host guests from all over the world.

Tinker's Bubble (England)

There's a saying in this UK community which goes: "Money poor, but happiness rich."

The people in this happy community live in shacks that are made of timber. The power for the village comes from "Bubblites", which supply the energy to light the place, charge the laptops of the residents and allow them to enjoy any other electrical appliances.

The people who live in this community earn their living by selling timber that they produce or by selling organic produce.

Since 1994, this fine community keeps growing and developing. Most of the life in this community is outdoors. It can be cold during the winter, but you can get warmer if you decide to live on a steep hill.

At this moment, there are only 11 adults and 2 young children who live there. They welcome new people who wish to start a new life in their community while following, respecting and accepting the community's practices and principles.

Lord Howe Island (Australia)

If you're planning to live off the grid for a short period of time, you may consider this amazing island.

People choose to come to this remote and secluded location in order to clear their minds, recharge with new energies and just get away and disconnect from the stress and noise of urban day to day living.

The current community in the island contains 350 residents who choose to live a peaceful living, embracing the off the grid lifestyle.

Vieques (Puerto Rico)

Vieques in Puerto Rico is another beautiful island. This island is also secluded and without a doubt a piece of paradise, where people choose to live their off the grid lifestyle.

Life on the island is a lot more relaxed and slower than modern city living. Vieques island is not crowded at all, it's lush and the nature here is stunningly beautiful. All that is left for you to do is to come here, disconnect yourself from modern society, maybe even turn off your phone and start enjoying this amazing paradise for an off grid way of life.

Freedom Cove (Canada)

Freedom Cove came to life thanks to artists Wayne and Catherine Adams. This off grid community is actually a floating world, and the two have worked really hard to make this possible. I am not completely sure whether you can join and be a part of their floating world, but there are boat tours available to the island, so that you can dock and then tour the place.

In the tour, you will visit the facilities and really learn how the two made their dream to live off the grid come true in such a unique way. You will also learn and enjoy the couple's art and understand how it is possible to live in such a remote location while floating on the water.

Tristan Da Cunha (UK)

Tristan Da Cunha (aka Tristan) is the best place if you're interested in isolation. Tristan contains 253 citizens from the UK who chose to live their lives off the grid and disconnect themselves from the busy and stressful urban lifestyle. It's a highly desirable destination for people who possess the escapist state of mind.

Easter Island (Polynesia)

Easter Island is a volcanic island that is suitable for those who wish to enjoy a lifestyle that is both eco-friendly and self-sufficient, yet don't want to commit to build their own home. This is more fitting for those who wish to tread lightly, who want some free time from their technological devices and simply recharge their minds and souls.

The island is known to have some of the best sunsets in the whole wide world. Also, you can visit the sculpture site on the island which consists of 900 statuses that were built between the 13th and 16th centuries.

The Azores (Portugal)

The Azores are located in the middle of the Atlantic. These islands are perfect for those who are looking for some piece of mind and quiet time. This is true especially due to the fact that not a lot of tourists have discovered the place yet.

The Azores are beautiful, and they are another potential paradise for your body and soul to recharge with new energies. Lonely Planet even mentioned that it's difficult to imagine a more suitable place for those who love nature, enjoy adventurous sport activities and basically anyone who is looking for a great time and quiet vacation.

Macquarie Island (Australia)

The plants and wild life on Macquarie Island are considered paradise for many biologists and botanists. The island and its waters have been declared a Tasmanian Nature Reserve. If that's not enough, this place is also home for a great population of the royal penguin.

The island also has a low population of people on it, which ranges from 20-40 people only at any given moment. This makes Macquarie Island ideal for those who are looking for off the grid quietness, while being surrounded by the island's stunning nature.

Barrow (Alaska)

Living in Barrow, Alaska, means living 100% off the grid. This means that in order to sustain yourself, you will need to forage, hunt and fish your own food. Therefore, moving there is a real adventure. So, if you're willing to join the lifestyle of the community in Barrow and provide your own food, this could be your next off the grid location, where you can start a new way of life.

Lammas Ecovillage (Wales)

Back in 2014, The Guardian voted Lammas Ecovillage in Wales as one of the top 10 best eco-homes in UK. If you wish to live the off the grid lifestyle as part of a community, this is the best place for you. Here, every single thing revolves around the community, and people are eager to help each other in times of need.

The people at Lammas work together to create as well as sustain a community that is self-reliant and land-based. So, if starting to live off the grid sounds a bit difficult to you, here you will be able to enjoy the help and support of this amazing community.

There are a few more astounding places to live off the grid in UK.

Konohana Family (Japan)

Konohana Family in Japan also centers on a community working together to achieve an off the grid way of life and sustain this lifestyle.

The people in this village are also very spiritual, as they aim to become a community that lives together and follows the law of the universe. Their goal is to use each other's talent in order to make the world a better, peaceful and more harmonious place.

False Kiva, Utah (USA)

The Canyonlands of the US have always been a favorite visiting place for people and hikers. The place is known for its breathtaking scenery. If you still haven't been there, it is a must place to visit.

False Kiva is located in one of the caves in the area and it is a stone circle that is man-made. You can reach and visit it only by hiking. We recommend that during the hike you leave your cell phone away and maybe even turn it off to fully absorb the surroundings and the nature around you.

Fernando De Noronha (Brazil)

Fernando De Noronha is a favorite vacation spot for many people from all over the world. If you only associate Brazil with carnivals and amazing beaches, then this place will give you a new perspective of Brazil.

The place has an ecological sanctuary where you can spot rays, dolphins, reef sharks and sea turtles through the clear and clean waters. Now, tell me that this isn't the best place to unwind, relax and enjoy nature at its finest.

Raoul Island (New Zealand)

Raoul Island is an excellent place for you if you really wish to dedicate your life to off grid living. New Zealand is known to be as one of the most beautiful places in the world, with views seemingly taken from artwork and some of the best mountainous backdrops you'll ever find. This island with all its nature may be the place for your off the grid lifestyle.

Khula Dhamma (South Africa)

Yes, even in Africa there is a place where you can embrace the off-the-grid lifestyle. Khula Dhamma is an ecovillage in South Africa containing natural homes, and the community there helps each other and sustains the off the grid living successfully.

Volunteers helped secure water supply to the village community by using a solar pump, setting up two beehives, a small garden, outdoor compost toilet, and more.

OFF GRID COMMUNITIES AROUND THE WORLD

Off grid communities have been around for decades, but they drew an increased attention and interest in the recent years. Social unrest, economic and political instabilities, natural disasters, unwelcome pandemics – everything that's been happening recently is driving people toward simpler and freer lifestyle.

I did an extensive research and made the most comprehensive list of such communities around the globe. Some of them were mentioned earlier in the book. Since this book is written in English, I mostly list the communities in the English-speaking countries, but I will mention off grid communities in other countries as well.

Off Grid Communities in USA

The United States has always been an encouraging nation, as far as off grid living is concerned. There are states such as Florida, Arizona, Colorado and Missouri, where the combination of climate, land availability and local laws creates very welcoming conditions to live off the grid.

- **Emerald Earth** in Mendocino County, California, is based on 189 acres of meadows and forest. The community was established in 1989 by their own non-profit organization. Like-minded individuals and families are invited to apply for membership. The community grows their own food and strives to enrich their environment instead of depleting it. Emerald Earth's members have an extensive knowledge of natural building and sustainable agriculture. They also conduct workshops, harvest seaweed at the coast and raise their own livestock. Although everyone involved do a lot of communal work, they also have plenty of spare time and energy for personal projects.

- **Dancing Rabbit Ecovillage** is an off-grid community located in the northeast part of Missouri. Dozens of its members enjoy living in houses made from recycled materials that are powered by renewable energy. This ecological village has been flourishing for over two decades. Visitors to Dancing Rabbit can gain a lot by learning organic gardening, production of alternative energy, self-governing management, and other useful off-grid skills. The ecovillage functions as a living laboratory, testing how permaculture can serve as a better approach to farming. The community also holds annual events, such as the Women's Retreat, singing gatherings and Open House, and everyone is invited to visit.
- **Earthaven** is a community based near Asheville, North Carolina, in the mountains. Established in 1995, they currently have about 100 residents. Their holistic approach to life and dedication to sustainable culture make Earthaven ecovillage a great place to visit or live in. The village is located on a biodiverse land and has dozens of homesteads, with more being built all the time. Like many other off grid communities, this one also takes care of ecological systems and operates by permacultural principles. There are many different people in Earthaven: some are vegetarians, while others are omnivores who raise livestock. The power is supplied by solar system installations.

- **Breitenbush** is a thriving community in the mountains of Oregon. They are truly off the grid, as the power is supplied by the river and by geothermal wells. The buildings are designed by the principles of sustainability and recycling. The lumber used is only from the trees that fell on their own or were struck down by the forces of nature. Breitenbush is a home to dozens of people and always welcomes visitors and tourists.
- **Three Rivers Recreation Area** is another large Oregon community. Its 600+ residents decided to completely go off the grid. You will not find a single power of phone line throughout its 4,000 acres. 450 houses are powered by solar energy, while the residents enjoy clear skies and a quiet atmosphere. It's a gated off grid community, so apply via their site if you wish to visit or move there. Nonetheless, this successful community is a real proof just how wonderful the off-grid style can be!
- **Twin Oaks** is a self-sufficient community in Virginia. It operates on the principles of income-sharing: all its members work in the community's businesses, and in return they receive clothing, food, housing, and so on. This intentional community exists since 1967, and it's completely free from centralized leadership. Today there are over 100 members living in Twins Oaks, and new members are encouraged to apply. To become a member, you first need to complete their Three-Week Visitor Period, in order to see whether this life of social cohesion and teamwork suits you. Visit their site for more information.
- **Freedom Village Georgia** is a modern off-grid eco-village. It's entirely self-contained, and is managed by the ideas outlined in "The Principles of Freedom" book. A co-living community in the very center of the state of

Georgia, it contains over 60 tiny houses, restaurants, art center, park and a lake. There are modern facilities as well, such as schools, medical center, shuttle service, internal hi-tech network, and so forth. This sustainable community has over 400 members, and always welcomes more members and visitors.

Off Grid Communities in Canada

The off-grid lifestyle is flourishing in Canada. Thousands of groups, families and individuals are settling on their own land, away from the bustling cities. The areas around Rocky Mountains, Okanagan Valley and New Brunswick are especially sought after. At the same time, other parts of Canada are less suitable for the off grid life, as I explained in an earlier chapter.

- **Lasqueti Island** is a community of 400 people, located in Vancouver's vicinity. The local residents' lifestyle is self-sufficient and totally off the grid. They prefer composting toilets and solar power to the modern appliances. It's a diverse community of individuals, many of whom are skilled at fishing, logging, planting, farming, manufacturing, and also making music, writing and creating in general. The community welcomes visitors, tourists and anyone who wished to temporarily or permanently experience this type of life. You can contact them via the site.
- **Terre de la Reunion** is a new community based in a mountain maple grove in Quebec. It was only recently established, but already has 13 buildings. The driving ideology of this community is peaceful co-existence of equal people. The residents are highly ecologically aware and always make sure that their actions never harm the nearby environment. Terre de la Reunion welcomes visitors and new members, but keep in mind that the community's daily language is French.
- **La Cité Écologique** is another community in Quebec.

This is an eco-village that covers 700 acres of land, with about 100 of them producing a wide range of crops. No chemicals were used on this property for over 35 years. The eco-village also offers full education of children. Visitors are welcome to visit the learning center, and there is always an option to become a new permanent member.

- **Freedom Cove** is a famous miniature off grid community, made from recycled platforms that simply float on the waters of the Cypress Bay, near the town of Tofino, BC. This artificial island was initially built by a couple of artists some 30 years ago, and today it includes a dance floor, greenhouses and an art gallery. The floating community constantly evolves, with new structures constantly being added to it. Everything here is made from a reclaimed material and inspired by nature. This complex home is not just off the grid, it's simply on nature's grid.

Off Grid Communities in United Kingdom

The off grid life in UK can be challenging, but then again, it's challenging in other places around the globe, too. You will need to locate an arable land, preferably close to a water source, so some scouting across the UK is in order. And unless you intend to dwell in a hut or a caravan, you will need to deal with UK Planning Permission System before establishing a permanent homestead. Here are a few off grid places in UK that make it work.

- **Brithdir Mawr** is a large farm in Pembrokeshire, West Wales. It does not use the country's water lines and power lines, therefore it's completely off the grid. The residents conserve and recycle resource, dedicate their time to organic farming and generally take care of the nature and the environment. There are currently 20 people living on an area of 165 acres, and they welcome visitors as well as new members. Adult members are required to work 3 days per week for the community, and the rest of their time can be directed to their personal projects. Brithdir Mawr's vision is to keep educating future generations regarding sustainable lifestyle and the preservation of natural resources.

- **Findhorn Foundation's Community Eco-Village Project** is located in the northeastern part of Scotland. There are over 400 people living here, from 40 different countries! Together, they participate in this huge experiment, running an intentional community, cooperating and creating together. The eco-village is open to more members and visitors from all over the world. The natural conditions at the Findhorn peninsula are challenging, yet the residents were able to establish beautiful gardens that flourish on the sand dunes. From its humble start as a caravan park, this community has significantly grown over the years, constantly evolving and expanding.
- **Tinkers Bubble**, situated in rural Somerset, England, is a charming woodland community that runs without any use of the fossil fuels. The small houses with thatched roofs create the illusion that you stepped into Tolkien's Shire. Nonetheless, this is a great off grid community with solid goals and principles. They make sure that their impact on the environment is minimal. They use compost toilets, spring water connected to the taps and solar energy. The small village always welcomes volunteers and curious visitors.

Off Grid Communities in Australia

Off grid living is definitely on the rise in Australia. People are drawn to the eco-friendly aspect of this life style, as well as more affordable housing costs. It's not illegal to live off the grid there, but some rules and limitations do apply. I have even more information in the separate chapter about living off the grid in Australia. And now, let's have a look at the local off grid communities.

- **Aldinga Arts EcoVillage** is a community located at 40km to the south of Adelaide, SA. Their main focuses are permaculture, environmental sustainability and arts. A truly cohesive community, Aldinga Arts EcoVillage sees its people as the most valuable asset. There are tons of group activities and projects open to everyone, including a small farm. It has over 400 members and invites everyone to visit or settle there. Their website lists houses that are currently available for renting or purchase.
- **Witchcliffe Ecovillage** is a brand new eco-village in Western Australia. It was planned for 10 years, and it's open for new settlers. The goal is to reach 1,000 residents, who will enjoy a peaceful life in a self-sustainable settlement. The eco-village intends to be highly affordable as well as green. Fresh food produce, renewable water, solar power – you name it. You can enjoy the benefits and comfort of modern life, while reducing your carbon footprint. The community will provide proper education, courses and workshop, which will teach you how water, food, waste and energy are handled within this village. This will help you become a full member in this unique off grid community.
- **BEND Eco-Neighbourhood** in Bega, NSW, is a neighborhood in a small Australian town that is entirely off the grid. They use solar hot water, passive solar design, rainwater and composting toilets. Currently there are 22 houses, with 10 available for cheap rent. There are plans to establish more households, as this community of 50 people intends to expand. The com-

munity stretches across an area of 10 hectares next to the Bega River, evenly split between agriculture, housing and reforestation purposes. There are a few vacant lots for sale as well, feel free to contact the community via their website.

- **Chewton Bushlands** started all the way back in 1967, when two people purchased land in central Victoria. Their initial plan was to establish a community of alternative lifestyle. 5 decades passed since then, and there are currently 35 households under Chewton Bushlands Association, who live there off the grid. Surrounded by the amazing bush flora and fauna, the residents make sure they preserve the nearby nature. The Chewtonians encourage the use of solar energy, organic farming and the spirit of community. Frequent events make the local life even more enjoyable and interesting. The community is open to new permanent and part-time members.

Off Grid Communities in New Zealand

New Zealand is a very appealing off-grid destination, thanks to its remoteness and the astonishing nature. Both the Tasman Sea shore and the West coast are suitable locations; especially the West coast, thanks to its richness of fresh water sources. There are a couple of off-grid NZ communities as well.

- **Kotare Village** is a community in Hawke's Bay Region. This eco-village is a home to dozens of self-reliant families, who want nothing more but to enjoy their independent life style as well as a regenerative future. Currently, their main power source is solar panels, and they plan to establish their own energy grid. The community's trust owns the land, so you never have to worry about the government reclaiming it. The village is planned to be sustainable for many years in the future, offering an alternative to the unstable global economy.

- **Te Manawa** is another eco-village, located in the Motueka Valley. This small and charming community always welcomes guests and volunteers. There is a scenic natural views wherever you look, with mountains, valley, sea and even 2 fresh springs nearby. There is a story about a Dutch family that fell in love with the place and completely relocated there. They now live in a yurt and enjoy every moment of this peaceful and fulfilling lifestyle. Everyone in the community feels like they are the guardians of this land. The power is supplied by solar and hydro systems. It's a completely sustainable eco-village that exists in harmony with the surrounding environment.
- **Wilderland** was established in 1964 on the Coromandel peninsula. It started as one of New Zealand's earliest organic farms, and eventually transformed into a well-known sustainable community. People who live or visit Wilderland learn significant skills that help them to practically and intelligently live off the land. The Wilderland Trust is always focused on developing both the land and the people tending to it. Wilderland carries experimentation that explores eco-balance while growing new crops and plants. On a more personal level, the local community encourages creativity and education, while discouraging any use of drugs and substances. This is truly a great place to be and grow.

Off Grid Communities in Other Countries

The off grid situation in other countries widely varies. Obviously, some of the countries are not yet fully modernized, so a large part of the local population already lives off the grid (if a grid even exists there). In other places, a strict religious or Communist regime does not allow any form of personal freedom.

This why I will mostly mention off grid communities in democratic countries.

- **Oasis du Coq à l'Âme** is a relatively new eco-community in Bordeaux region, France. They choose to govern themselves by the method of holacracy, a system of decentralized management that does not recognize a hierarchy of managers, and is comprised of self-organizing teams instead. The community promotes the principles of energetic simplicity, food autonomy and shared governing system. They are approximately 20 families, and they wholeheartedly welcome new members and visitors. This is a pilot village, a part of the Oasis program inspired by the Colibri movement. The community is open to the world, and they firmly believe in their philosophy and goals.
- **Villa Monte Reserve** in northwestern Argentina is a communal place that embraces both people and the nature. 400 acres of native forest, plus rivers, plus caves, plus springs, and so forth – this is truly a place to live in! This small yet beautiful community always welcomes visitors, new members and new ideas. It's a private natural reserve that contains unique fauna and flora, thanks to its being a midway zone between several ecosystems. The local people promote conservation of the forest and its biodiversity, organic farming and sustainable lifestyle.
- **Global Tribe Biodynamic Eco-village** is located next to the Doñana National Park in southern Spain. It's a very astounding place, approximately situated between two countries, two continents and two large bodies of water (the Atlantic Ocean and the Mediterranean Sea). There are plenty of beautiful and historical places in the vicinity to hike. The community itself adheres to biodynamism, growing and harvesting the crops according to the natural cycles, as well as by

using only natural fertilizers and pesticides. They welcome new members and open to visitors.

- **Monte dos Carvalhos** (Mount of Oaks) is a small off-grid community in the municipality of Fundão, Portugal. It's a very tranquil place, with kind people whose sole focus is to care for the land, plants and animals. They frequently hold workshops, teaching the best and most natural ways of agriculture. They are also open to new member and visitors, offering a safe and quiet space to anyone who seeks it.
- **Catfarm** is an open off-grid community near the village of Poussan, France, close to the coast of the Mediterranean Sea. They embrace alternative ways of life and welcome free and creative spirits. They constantly run new projects, while teaching the local folks better methods of waste-reduction, land cultivation and creative expression. You can stay as a new member or as a guest, by renting a tipi or parking your RV. The Catfarm is a fun and nurturing place to truly experience the off-grid life.

PART 3: PRACTICAL GUIDES AND INFORMATION

OFF GRID VS ON GRID SOLAR

I have extensively discussed where you should live off the grid. Now let's transition to the "how" and see what practical knowledge you must have before establishing your off the grid homestead.

Solar panels are often considered the basics of living off the grid. You produce your own electricity, independently of the country's power grid. However, recent years saw many solar system owners becoming interested in the on grid option. So, before getting to the practical guides, I decided to "shine some light" on the differences between the two approaches.

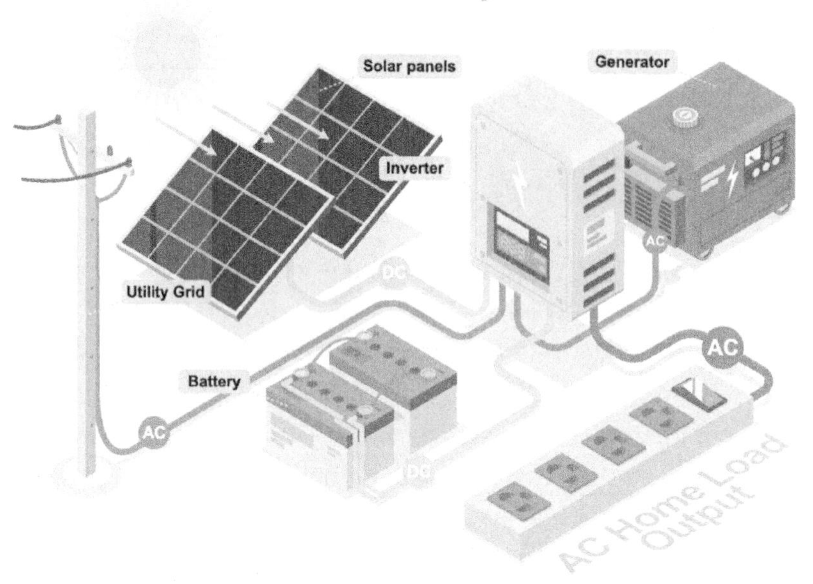

The Off Grid Solar System in a Nutshell

There are many reasons for having off grid power. You want a greener energy source. You want to feel independent. You live far away from everything, can't hook up to the big power grid and a generator is costly, noisy and polluting.

In any of these cases, **the sun becomes your energy provider**. You install solar panels that convert the sunbeams to electricity. They actually do not cost as much as they used to. You will also need a DC to AC inverter, since the panels produce direct current (or DC), while your appliances usually require the AC electricity (if they connect to the outlet).

Here is where it gets tricky. If you're dreaming about going completely off grid, keep in mind that the sun is not beaming on a daily basis. You will need a backup for the literal rainy day.

Some folks go for the aforementioned generator, many however purchase a reliable batter bank. Whichever you choose, that's an additional cost to your setup.

The Advantages of the On Grid Solar System

The on grid solution is also called grid-tied system, since it's actually connected to the power grid. Yes, you are not entirely unplugged and free as you imagined. However, in some scenarios, this system has noticeable advantages.

1. You are covered on the sunless days. The utility hook-up will provide you with the power you're currently lacking.
2. Therefore, you will not need to invest into the backup battery or generator.
3. If you're producing excess electricity, it is fed back into the grid (instead of being stored in a battery). By the end of the year, you cash out whatever you've "donated". That's right, **the power company could pay you back**. But be sure to check with them first, as the buy-back option is not always available in every area.

A possible disadvantage is when the power grid is down due to some technical difficulties. Without the back battery, you could be sitting in the dark.

Introducing a Third Solar System - Hybrid

The hybrid solar system unites the two previously mentioned options. It's grid-tied just like the on grid system, but it also has a battery, similar to the off grid solution. However, the battery can be much smaller and cheaper. You use both the sun and the local power grid to your advantage without investing too much money into the whole setup.

The hybrid solar system has also created a need for a new type of inverters. You can **control when you output the energy to your devices**, when you collect it into the battery bank, and when you give it to the utility grid. Thus, you can flexibly take advantages of the electricity rates that vary in different hours of the day. Use the gird when it's the cheapest, send them the extra watts when they pay the most.

Side note: there is a different kind of a hybrid that exists, a system that combines both solar energy and wind power. You can read more about this interesting and efficient option further down this chapter.

Off Grid VS On Grid VS Hybrid Solar – The Verdict

The following table compares between the three systems.

	Off Grid	On Grid	Hybrid
Connects to grid	No	Yes	Yes
Requires battery	Yes	No	Yes
Possible cash-out	No	Yes	Yes
Cost	Moderate to high	Low	Moderate

Decide for yourself which one works for you. Among the factors that should influence your decision are:

- Budget
- Local weather
- Distance to the utility hook-up
- Power company's willingness to pay you back

Do You Really Save Money with Solar Panels?

In the (not so) long run, you do save a lot of money. But don't take my word for it. Take a look at your utility bills and check the local rates. Getting solar panels might just be the thing you need. Not convinced yet? Then know that:

1. The installation of the solar system has actually become cheaper in the recent years.
2. The energy costs, on the other hands, are not going

down any time soon.

3. You get a significant **tax deduction**. The so called federal solar tax credit grants you a tax break of 30% of the installation's price. Whether you live off the grid in the USA or enjoy Canadian off the grid living, check if these tax credits apply to you.
4. The solar panels last a long time and don't demand a lot of maintenance and replacement.
5. And just face it, a greener, less polluted environment also saves money in a variety of ways!

Can I Add Solar Panels to My Existing System?

Extra solar panels can be easily added, which can be useful in the following cases:

1. Your current on grid setup satisfies your needs, and now you intend to give something back to the power company in exchange for a payment.
2. Contrarily, you want to go completely off grid. You will need a bigger battery, and more panels are needed to fill it up.
3. You have a lot of unused space of your rooftop, and the thought of all that sunlight being wasted keeps you up at night.
4. Your current inverter is too big for the energy that you produce, and you decide to take full advantage of its capacity. However, **carefully check its capabilities**. Upgrade your system according to specifications of your inverter's MPPT inputs. Use panels with precisely the same amperage and voltage that your inverter can deal with.

Additional Ways to Use the Sun's Power and Cut Costs

If you're looking to cut costs, consider **thermal water heating system**. It is somewhat similar to the panel, but instead of transforming the solar rays to electrical power, it traps and uses them to produce heat. The heat is carried to the water tank, and there you have it, hot water for everyone in your house. Your electrical bill will feel much lighter thanks to this invention.

There is also the **passive solar design**, a method that is both simple and ingenious. Basically, parts of the house itself can be used to either heat or cool it by using the sun itself and not a watt of electricity. This system does not require a lot of moving or mechanical parts. The common varieties are:

1. Windows – strategically placed and easily opened to provide the necessary temperature.
2. Thermal chimney – it forces the heat to rise, thus making the air move and cool the house.
3. Thermal mass – parts of the building (bricks, walls, floor) or big water containers that stockpile the heat for long periods of time.

SOLAR POWER

Off grid solar systems are quite easy to set up. You can get the equipment from a local store and use common hand tools to put the solar system together at home.

The components that you require to set up a working off-grid solar power system successfully are:

- Solar panels
- Battery pack
- Solar inverter or solar charge controller
- Battery inverter or multimode inverter
- Wiring equipment

What to consider when choosing the equipment for your off-grid solar setup

The equipment you need for installation depends on the amount of power you consume, the number of electrical appliances you have, and the amount of time you have them running. The calculation for power requirement at your home involves estimating the amount of time that you have each appliance running and multiplying that by its power consumption rating.

To get the total amount of power you need for your home, begin by estimating each electric appliance's power consumption and adding up each value to get the total load requirement. The solar power system equipment installed should match the load requirement. Installing a system with less power than the load requirements leads to the equipment being overwhelmed and power running out before the end of the day. On the other hand, systems with large power capacity are expensive and installing them in homes with little power requirement is not economical.

Choosing equipment

After estimating the load capacity, the next step is choosing equipment that can match the load requirements. The section below goes into detail on what to consider when picking each of the equipment required to set up a solar power system.

Picking a solar panel

The solar panel is the equipment that is exposed to sunlight and is where the whole process of power generation begins. Solar panels have Photovoltaic (pv) cells on the surface that convert the rays of sunlight to electric direct current (DC). Solar panels have multiple cells that are linked together and use different methods of cell arrangement, which allows placement of multiple cells on the surface.

Solar panels are available with mono cell arrangement, half cut cell arrangement, shingled cell arrangement, or busbar cell arrangement. The bottom of the solar panel has wire connectors that transfer the generated power.

Solar panels are rated according to the amount of DC current they produce after being exposed to sunlight for a period of time. You, therefore, should buy solar panels that can charge your battery pack fully in one day. Remember to take into consideration that sunlight changes intensity during the day and that the panel is not exposed to sunlight throughout the day. So, it is better to pick solar panels that have a slightly higher rating than is required to charge the battery.

Picking a battery pack

The battery pack is important in a solar power system setup because it enables storage of charge for use when there is no sunlight. The battery also helps in stabilizing the power before it is consumed by any electrical appliance. It is worth noting that the solar panel does not produce stable electricity due to changes in sunlight intensity at different times.

The various kinds of batteries available in the market have different capacities for storage. For a long time, people have been using car batteries to store power from solar panels. Car batteries are designed to supply short bursts of high current and do not perform well when discharged deeply. Solar batteries that are designed for deep discharge cycles are available and include the following types.

Lead-Acid Batteries

Lead-acid batteries are durable and offer the convenience of deep -discharge cycles, which means that you can use the battery until it almost discharges completely. This prevents frequent charging and discharging cycles that cause the battery to wear out. Lead acid batteries require one to keep them at temperatures below 104 degrees Fahrenheit to enable them to last for a long time. The batteries also require a regular charging cycle and temperature sensors to monitor and regulate voltage during charging.

Lead-acid batteries are recommended for use because they can be used until they fully run out of charge. Unlike Li-ion batteries, lead-acid batteries do not suddenly shut down. They are also compatible with most available inverters.

Lithium ion batteries

Lithium ion batteries are compact, which makes them portable. Compared to the other kinds of batteries, they are smaller, lighter, and have high efficiency. The time taken to charge a lithium-ion battery pack fully is also shorter as compared to lead-acid batteries, which makes them perfect for off-grid solar power setups.

Due to the technology used to manufacture lithium-ion batteries, they also do not suffer from sulfation, which is a common problem with lead-acid batteries.

Lithium-ion batteries require compatible inverters for them to work in a solar power setup. They also tend to shut down without warning when running low on charge or when they heat up to temperatures above 45oC.

Picking a battery for an off-grid setup requires selecting a battery that holds enough charge to power all the appliances until the next charge cycle. This typically means that the pack must hold enough charge to power all equipment overnight so that the battery can be recharged the next day.

Picking a Solar charge controller

A solar charge controller works to regulate how the battery pack is charged. As stated in the section above, solar panels have a varied DC current output that is dependent on the intensity of the sunlight that the panels receive. The charge controller regulates the current used to charge the battery by maintaining it at optimum levels to prevent overcharging. The rating for a charge controller is based on the charging requirements for the battery.

Picking an inverter

Solar panels use photovoltaic cells to convert sunlight to electrical power in the form of direct current (DC). Solar batteries also store charge that is supplied in form of DC current. Many appliances, however, use alternating current (AC), which is the common form of power supply on the grid. The inverter, therefore, receives DC current from the battery pack or solar panel and converts it to AC for use by electrical appliances.

Multimode inverters

Modern solar power setups have inverters that double up as AC/DC inverters and solar charge controllers. Multimode inverters help to monitor how the batteries are charged and manage power sources and backup power equipment.

As such, you need to consider picking an advanced inverter if you have equipment that requires non-stop power supply, such as an air conditioner.

Wiring equipment

You will need wiring equipment to connect the devices so that current can flow from the solar panel to the electrical appliances. Wiring equipment comprises the connectors to each device and the safety gadgets, such as fuses.

The connecting wires you pick should also be thick enough to carry enough current to all the appliances.

Setting up the Solar Power System

After purchasing all the necessary equipment, follow these steps to set up your solar power system.

Installing Solar Panels

The common place for installing the solar panels is the roof of your house. Roofs on most houses are slightly slanted, which makes them the perfect place for mounting the solar panels in order for them to receive maximum sunlight. Placing the solar panels on the roof also ensures that there are no objects that block the panels from the sun.

Some of the setups that use up more panels than the roof can hold have the panels mounted on the ground with the surface slightly angled towards the sky. For this setup, the panels should be placed on an open ground that has no obstructing objects, such as trees or tall plants.

Mounting the frame

Panels are sold with mounting frames that hold them firmly in place. The mounting frame should be angled between 18 and 36 degrees to enable the panels to enjoy maximum exposure to the sun.

Installing the panel

Once the mounting frames are securely installed, the panels should be placed in the frame and screwed down firmly using the nuts and bolts that come with the panel.

Wiring the solar panel

The next step is to connect the solar panels using wire connectors. MC4 connectors are commonly used since they fit most solar panels. Ensure that there are no exposed wires and that you test each joint connection after you finish wiring the panels.

Installing the inverter

The next step is installing the inverter. The ideal placement for the inverter is near the solar panel and at a place with sufficient airflow. You can also decide to place the inverter indoors, but ensure that the room where you mount it has sufficient ventilation openings. This is because inverters are sensitive to temperature and work best when cool. Exposure to hot direct sunlight could cause the inverter to malfunction.

Installing the battery

The inverter is then connected to the battery connectors to enable it to charge the battery. Before connecting them, however, ensure that the inverter and battery are compatible if you are using a Li-ion battery. Lead-acid batteries are usually compatible with most inverters.

Connecting the inverter and battery to the consumer unit

Next, connect the inverter to the consumer unit, which then distributes current to all the electrical outlets. The consumers unit allows you to install additional monitoring equipment that helps you to measure the performance of the solar power system.

Testing the solar power system

After all the components are connected, the next step involves testing the system to ensure that everything works. You have to leave enough time between when installation is completed and when you begin testing to allow the battery to be charged sufficiently. Testing should be done with small electrical appliances that consume little amount of power.

Maintenance tips for an off grid solar power system

Once the solar power system has been setup, you will need to perform regular maintenance. The section below discusses the maintenance tips for each equipment.

Maintaining solar panels

Solar panels are designed to withstand brutal weather conditions. The flat surface and slanted installation mechanism enable them to receive maximized exposure to the sun's rays and enables raindrops and debris to roll off from their surfaces easily. Periodic maintenance, however, is required during extreme weather such as the winter season when there is heavy snowfall.

Long dry spells with no rainfall also result in the surface of the solar panel accumulating dust, which can block the photovoltaic cells from sunlight. During such times, a quick spray of water on the panels' surfaces is needed.

When cleaning the panels, ensure that you do not spray cold water on the hot surface of the solar panel. This is because the rapid temperature change could damage the surface by causing it to contract quickly. Only warm water should be used to clean up the panel surface. Panels mounted the ground are easy to maintain since they are easier to access as compared to solar panels mounted on the roof.

Maintaining off grid solar system batteries

Battery maintenance enables you to get the most out of the battery. Following proper charging, storage and care tips ensures the battery remains in good working condition for a long time.

Lead-acid batteries are prone to sulfation, which occurs when the batteries have low charge or are low on electrolyte. Sulfation restricts the battery from charging up fully, which in turn results in faster discharging.

Charging batteries

Batteries can be charged using three charging methods. The first is trickle charging where the battery is charged at the same rate that it is discharging. This keeps the battery fully charged at all times. The second method is bulk charging. This charging method raises the held charge to the maximum level that the battery can hold. The third method is absorption charging that involves holding the voltage at one level and then dropping the current gradually until the battery is fully charged. Adjustable charge controllers allow you to set optimal voltage for bulk, absorption, and trickle charging.

Cleaning batteries

Batteries require regular cleaning to ensure that the terminals have maximum contact with the cable connection. The terminals can be cleaned using a mixture of distilled water and baking soda. Before working on them, ensure that the terminals have been disconnected.

Maintaining inverters and solar chargers

Solar inverters and chargers have small electrical components that are extremely sensitive. This means that high temperature levels could cause the components to malfunction. As a result, the inverters and charges should be placed in well-ventilated rooms. Inverters that are placed outside should be shielded to protect them from the damages caused by rain or falling hailstones. Shielding them also ensures that they are not exposed to direct sunlight that could heat them up and compromise their functionality.

Top five recommended solar systems

Generating your own electrical power is a great way to go if you are looking to achieve energy independence. Picking the right solar system to generate power for your home is dependent on the amount of power you consume. Check out the products that we recommend in this section since they are easy to install and maintain.

Grape Solar GS-400-Kit off-grid Solar panel kit

The Grape solar kit is a standalone fully equipped solar system kit. The kit comprises four mono-crystalline solar panels that can generate enough energy to power bulbs and small electrical equipment. The panels have an included junction box with LED lights that work to improve the kit's performance.

The kit includes a 35-amp charge controller and an inverter with an output rating of 2000 watts. The inverter also features twin standard AC power outlets and a USB cable that you can use to charge your handheld devices. The kit, however, does not include a battery pack; you need to purchase one if you need to store power for later use.

PeakSolar 10,000W complete photovoltaic system

PeakSolar 10,000W complete photovoltaic system is a grid tied system that provides enough electrical energy for all appliances in large houses. As such, it can be used to power an entire home. Moreover, the system can be set-up to provide backup power for small business premises when power from the grid-system is not available.

The system comes with 250-watt polycrystalline solar

panels that are designed for rooftop mounting and are accompanied by trucking and mounting equipment that help in setting up the system. The solar panels are made of poly-silicon material and the surface on each panel features micro inverts that work to maximize power conversion by reducing mismatch loss. Correct mounting of the solar panels using the included mounting equipment also guarantees wind resistance up to 2400 Pa and snow loads up to 5400 Pa. The manufacturer provides an SMA inverter with every purchase and covers the system with a 25-year warranty.

SolarPod Standalone modular system, 960 Watts, off-grid

This system has four crystalline solar panels with a combined output of 960 watts and is sold with four batteries for power storage. Also included in the system is a sine wave inverter. The system is scalable and allows additional panels to be installed.

The manufacturer covers this system under a 25-year limited warranty. The system is easy to install since the solar panels fit on racks and require no special brackets to hold them in place. The system is compatible with 120 volts and 240 volts' setups and is available for purchase on Amazon.

RENOGY Solar panel kit 400W, off-grid, with mounting brackets

RENOGY solar kit comprises of four 100-watt solar panels that are rated A for energy efficiency. The kit is sold with Z-shaped brackets that hold the panels at an optimum exposure angle and can be mounted on a flat surface. Moreover, it can be taken on the road to provide off-grid energy enough to power essential appliances such as computers, refrigerators, fans, and light bulbs.

The solar panels in this kit withstand brutal weather and produce enough power even in low sunlight. However, the kit does not include batteries for power storage, which means that you have to purchase them separately.

Eco-Worthy 1000W, 10 pieces, Solar module for homes

This kit includes 10 100-watt solar panels that have a combined power output of 1000 watts. The kit also comes with 10 180-centimetre long solar cables and 10 MC4 extensions. The polycrystalline solar panels have an inbuilt bypass diode that negates the shadow effect on the panels allowing conversion of sunlight into electric power even in low sunlight. This system's power output can power medium sized electrical appliances such as the microwave, fridge, lighting bulbs, and pumps.

The panels come with an IP-65 rated junction box that is waterproof and weather-resistant enabling the solar panels withstand heavy rainfall and snow. A heavy gauge aluminum frame that surrounds the solar panels also protects them from corrosion.

HYDROPOWER

Solar power is what comes to everyone's mind when they think about clean alternative energy. However, there are additional options. You can harness the elements and produce electricity from other sources, not just the sun. In this chapter, we will take a look at the hydropower, producing energy from flowing water.

Before we proceed, an important warning. I constantly mention the local laws throughout the book. You must check with the local authorities whether or not the usage of the hydropower is allowed in your area.

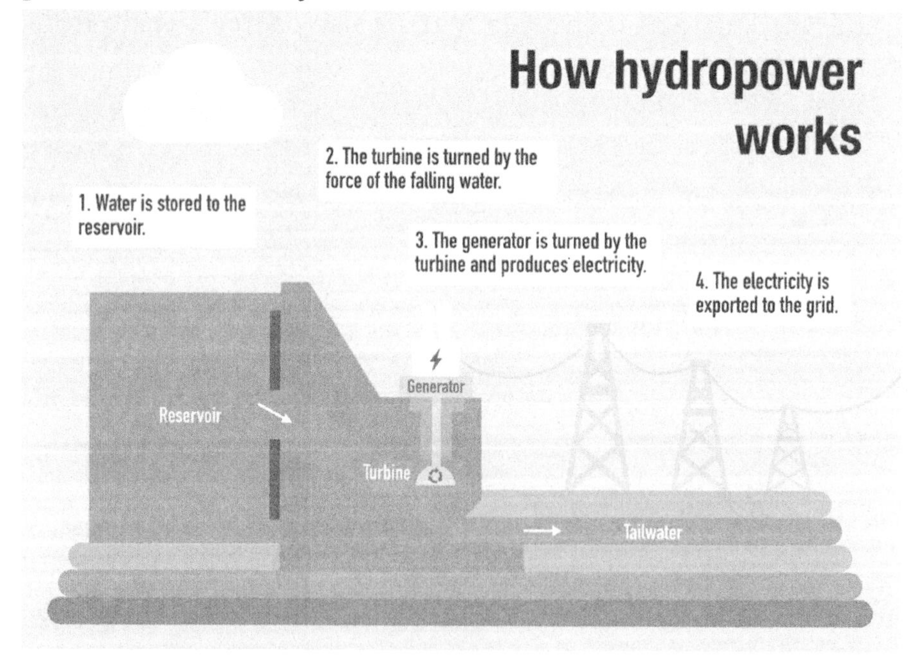

Microhydropower System

If there is a river or even a small spring flowing through your land, then you're in luck. You can use it to generate electricity. Just install a microhydropower system and enjoy hundreds of kW of free electrical energy. This can be enough to power up a large home or even a farm.

How does it work? Basically, in the center of a hydropower system is a waterwheel, pump or turbine. This part is moved by the flowing water, and then the rotation is transformed into electricity.

Additionally, a microhydropower system includes a generator or alternator, where this rotating movement is actually translated into energy. The generator/alternator is controlled by a regulator. Wiring is the final part of this system, it delivers electricity wherever it's needed.

It's important to mention that while sometimes the waterwheel is partially submerged into the water stream, usually there is a channel or a pipeline that brings the water from the natural stream and onto the wheel, pump or turbine.

You can purchase generators and turbines in one package. If you buy them separately, remember to match the generator and turbine's horsepower and speed with the greatest care possible.

Then there is also the issue of DC/AC. You can either get appliances that run on DC electricity, since this is what the hydropower system produces, or add an inverter to the system. The inverter will transform the low-voltage DC electrical power into 120 V or 140 V of AC electricity.

As for storing the produced electricity in batteries, it is less practical in the case of hydropower. The hydropower tends to be even more seasonal than solar or wind power. If you do choose to use batteries, install them in the turbine's vicinity, since low voltage power has difficulties being transmitted over a distance.

Since a waterwheel, pump or turbine is a central part of the system, let's quickly review them and list their advantages and disadvantages:

- **Waterwheel**: A waterwheel is the original system component, it's been around for many years. While waterwheels can still be obtained, they are not recommended. Their large size and slow velocity are less than ideal when it comes to producing electricity.
- **Pump:** Pumps, on the other hand, are more mass produced that any turbine. They usually don't cost much. When their functioning is reversed, they act just like a turbine. However, they are more breakable, less efficient and demand a constant flow of water in order to perform in a satisfactory manner.
- **Reaction turbine**: This extremely efficient type of turbine produces energy by pressure, as its blades are directly pushed by the water at all times. The reaction turbines are frequently used in large hydropower systems and are less common in microhydropower setups due to their cost.

  The only exception is a propeller turbine, which is more affordable. It works similarly to a boat's propeller and has 3-6 blades. The blades are set on the runner at different angles. A Kaplan turbine is a subtype of a propeller turbine, it's very adaptable and can be utilized in a microhydropower system.
- **Impulse turbine**: This type of a turbine has a relatively simple design and can be frequently found in high-head systems. They are operated by the water's velocity, which moves the runner (the turbine's wheel). There are several subtypes of the impulse turbine.
  - **Jack Rabbit turbine**: A small turbine, it actually requires only a foot of water depth. The output is 100 W, so thoroughly check if this is sufficient to power your household.

- **Pelton wheel**: The energy is created by jet force principle. The water goes into a pipeline with a narrow exit opening, formed like a nozzle. The water comes out of the nozzle in a jet, hitting the wheel's buckets. The buckets are formed to maximize the impact's influence, and the jet rotates the Pelton wheel with about 80% of efficiency. A Pelton wheel can be found in a variety of sizes and it's highly recommended for high-head, low-flow settings.
- **Turgo impulse wheel**: This is an improved Pelton wheel. The jet is smaller and angled, and it hits 3 buckets at the same time (and not 2, like in Pelton's case). This makes the wheel move at double speed. Turgo impulse wheel is known to be reliable and low-maintenance. It's smaller and includes less gears, or none at all.

Head and Flow

I mentioned "head" and "flow", but what exactly do they mean? They are the factors that you need to check in order to determine whether or not you have a suitable microhydropower site on your property. Just having a flowing water is not enough, although, of course, it's a great start. The water must fall, and its head and flow will tell you a lot about its energy-producing potential.

So, to put it simply:
Head is the vertical distance that the water falls.
Flow is how much water is falling.

Now, most microhydropower systems have around 53% efficiency. A simple formula can calculate the output you will have for such a system given the head and flow of your site. I'm using US measurement units for this formula, feel free to convert to your country's units. Net head is the vertical distance minus the pipe friction.

Net head (in feet) X Flow (in gallons per minute) / 10 = System's output (in Watts)

Let's discuss the measurement of these deciding factors. As you probably understand, higher head is preferable, since less water will be required to fall to produce enough energy, thus you'll need to install cheaper and smaller hydropower system. A high head is a vertical fall over 10 feet (or 3 meters). Anything less is considered a low head. And finally, a drop of less than 2 feet makes a typical microhydropower system completely impractical. In such cases you will need something like the aforementioned Jack Rabbit turbine, which is completely submersed into the water.

How do you get a rough estimate of head? You can either consult the geological maps of the area, or try the proven hose/tube method. The latter method will help to determine the distance between the potential penstock location and potential turbine placement. Get someone to help you and pack a funnel, a measuring tape (or a yardstick) and at least 8 feet of a small-diameter garden hose or any other flexible tube.

1. Stretch the tubing down the stream from the most practical elevation point for the penstock intake. Have your helper hold the upstream end of the hose underwater (with the funnel in it) as close to the surface as possible.
2. At the same time, lift the downstream end until water no longer flows from it. Measure the vertical distance between your end of the tube and the surface of the water. This is the gross head for that section of the stream.
3. Ask your helper to move to your current location and place the funnel there. Then walk downstream and repeat the procedure, measuring again. Continue taking measurements in this fashion until you reach the spot

where you intend to situate your turbine.

4. Summarize all these measurements, and you get the gross head available for your future hydropower system. If you're satisfied with the number, perhaps you should get a professional survey.

And what about flow? You can measure it as well. Naturally, to get a precise assessment, it is advisable that you contact the Department of Agriculture, the US Geographical Survey, your county's engineer or any other official specialist. That said, there are a couple of simple methods to measure your flow without contacting the authorities, at least to get some primary assessment.

The bucket method is the simplest way imaginable. Dam the stream with some boards and divert into a bucket or a similar container. Time how long it takes for the water to fill the bucket. The bucket's volume divided by the time it takes to completely fill it is the flow number.

A more advanced measurement method is performed with a weighted float. Be careful not to use it if the stream is too fast or too deep. Get someone to help you and pack a weighted float (for instance, a plastic bottle half-filled with water), some graph paper, a tape measure, a yardstick and a stop watch. The method helps to estimate flow at the lowest level of the streambed.

1. Select a section of stream with the straightest channel, and the most uniform width and depth.
2. At the narrowest point, measure the stream's width.
3. Hold the yardstick vertically, cross the stream and measure the water depth at every one foot. You can stretch a rope with the increments marked on it.
4. Use the graph paper to plot the depths. This is the cross-sectional profile of the stream.
5. Determine the sections' areas. To do this, calculate the areas of the rectangles (area = length X width) and triangles (area = base X height divided by 2). Do this for every section.

6. Mark a point at least 20 feet upstream from the point where you measured the width..
7. Set the weighted float free in the middle of the stream. Time with the stopwatch how long it takes for the float to reach the initial point downstream. If the float drags against the bottom, use a smaller one.
8. Now you can divide the distance between the points by the time in seconds. You get the flow velocity in feet per second. Repeat this procedure several times to get even more precise measurement. Calculate the average velocity.
9. Next, multiply this velocity by the cross-sectional area that you measured earlier.
10. Finally, multiply the result by the factor of roughness. Different stream channels have different roughness factors: 0.8 for a sandy streambed, 0.7 for a bed with small to medium stones, 0.6 for a streambed with numerous large stones. This final result will give you the flow rate in cubic feet (or meters) per second.

Keep in mind that the flow is often seasonable. When you design your system, take the lowest average flow, to be on the safe side. On the other hand, the local laws might restrict you on how much water you're allowed to divert at different seasons. In this case, take the average flow rate from the period of the highest demand for electricity.

WIND POWER

The potential in harnessing the wind power to make clean electricity is enormous. If your off-grid property has the right conditions and resources, seriously consider installing a small wind electric system. It has no pollutions and emissions, and all in all is a great source of renewable and free energy.

While the common electric grid can be costly and is prone to outages, especially in remote areas, the reliable and constant wind power can reduce your bills by as much as 90%. You can use it to power your entire home, as well as your farm's water pumps and irrigation systems.

So does it work? Basically, our sun heats the earth's surface unequally, thus creating wind. A wind turbine takes the wind's kinetic energy and transforms it into electricity. When the blades of the turbine are spun by the wind, a rotor takes this energy and converts into rotary motion that drives the generator.

Many turbines take this system even further and include an automatic overspeed component that deals with high winds. And finally, this setup is either connected by wires to the power provider's grid, or in our case, directly to the off-the-grid household.

Is Your Area Suitable for a Small Wind Electric System?

Before we even discuss the environment of your property, let's mention the zoning and permitting issues. Before even considering to install a wind electric system, learn about the local restrictions and consult with the local building inspectors or supervisors. You might need to acquire a building permit.

Additionally, if you live closer to other people, both your neighbors and the laws might object to certain aspects of the wind turbine and its tower. A high tower can obstruct the view, many residential areas insist that the tower's height shouldn't exceed 35 feet.

And then there is the noise issue. Usually the sound that a modern wind turbine makes is no louder than the wind itself. This means that you don't have to worry that you or your neighbors will be bothered by the noise, but always check whether the turbine's make is considered quiet before you purchase it.

And now to the environment itself. How good is the wind resource in your vicinity? The terrain around you can affect the wind a lot. The wind flow at your location might be quite different from the one only a couple of miles way. Naturally, there are ways to be certain.

- **Wind resource map**: Yes, such a thing exists. If you live in the USA, there is the Wind Powering America Program maintained by the Department of Energy. It makes map for every state, and you can consult them to see exactly how the wind blows in your area.
- **Vegetation flagging**: Strong winds affect the vegetation and can provide a strong visual cue regarding the wind speeds around you. For instance, particularly strong winds can noticeably deform the evergreen and conifer trees. This is called "flagging".
- **Local wind systems**: An obvious solution, see if there are turbines in your area and get the information from their operators and owners. Ask them how much a system can output in a year, given the local wind speeds.
- **Airport**: Another potential source of valuable information can be a nearby airport, where they usually track the wind speeds. However, keep in mind that the data does not necessarily reflect the terrain around your household. Also, the airports measure the winds

at the average height of 25 feet, while a typical wind tower can be about 80 feet, and the winds at that height are about 20% stronger.

- **Measurement system**: A do-it-yourself method. To be on the safe side, you can invest about $500 - $1300 into a wind measurement equipment and get a clear picture of the wind resource at your property. This equipment will need to be raised high enough to avoid any obstruction caused by trees, buildings and such – in other words, at the future wind turbine's height.

Once you're satisfied with the wind resource, you will need to decide on the exact site for the wind turbine. The turbine's manufacturer should be able to help you with this decision. First, there should be enough room around the site if the turbine's tower needs to be lowered and raised for installation and maintenance. Many towers come with guy wires (see below), so there also must be enough room for those. And then there is the electrical wiring, connecting the turbine and the place it serves, such as the house or farming equipment. A long wire causes great losses to the electricity, especially if it's DC. If a long wire can't be avoided, then invert DC to AC first.

The terrain's peculiarities should be also taken into consideration, if you want to make the most of the available wind resource. For instance, if you have a hill, you can install the tower on its top or on its windy side. You must also know the direction in which the wind blows most of the time before making the siting decision. Nearby trees and houses (current or planned to be built in the future) can be an obstacle. The rule of the thumb is that the turbine should be located upwind of any obstacle, and should be 30 feet higher than anything within a radius of 300 feet.

What Are the Wind Systems Made of?

I briefly mentioned earlier some of the components of a typical wind power system, but let's take a closer look so that you become more familiar with them.

A **turbine** is usually an upwind machine with horizontal axis. It comes with 2-3 blades made from fiberglass or some other composite material. The turbine's tail, generator and rotor are attached to its frame. The rotor's diameter determines just how much energy is produced. A larger rotor, of course, intercepts more wind. The tail part is what ensures that the turbine faces into the blowing wind.

The turbine is mounted on a **tower**, since the wind speed is higher when you get further away from the ground. You can invest an insignificant amount of money to get an even higher tower, and this investment will quickly pay off thanks to the higher rates of power production. For instance, doubling the tower height can add only about 10% to the total cost of the system, but the power production will be higher by 25%!

The towers are often included in the manufactures systems. There are two types, free-standing (self-supported) towers and guyed towers (steadied by cords or cables). Guyed towers can sometimes come in a tilt-down version. Guyed towers are more common in home wind systems, since they are noticeably cheaper and can be easy to install. Keep in mind that the guy radius is about 1/2 to 3/4 of the tower's height, so make sure you have enough space for the entire structure.

The tilt-down version costs more, but if you're running a lightweight, small turbine (about 10 kW), then you can enjoy the advantage of much easier maintenance. Additionally, if a hurricane strikes your area, this type of a tower can be quickly lowered to the ground.

Last word on towers – stay away from the aluminum ones. They crack too easily.

The rest of the parts depend on your wind electric system's application. The parts needed for a home power supply are not the same as required for water pumps and agriculture. Moreover, the parts depend on whether it's an off-grid, on-grid or hybrid system.

The wind systems are usually manufactured with everything you need for your own application. In other words, you don't need to think too hard what parts you must purchase. For example, if you plan to connect your wind system to your house, you can get a package that has all the appropriate parts:

- Tower foundation
- Grounding system
- Wiring
- Disconnect switch
- Inverter
- Storage batteries
- Controller

Installation and Maintenance

Installation of a wind power system is a challenging issue for a single, untrained person. I would strongly advise that you let the dealer or the manufacturer do all the heavy lifting. The installation requires pouring cement foundation, safely erecting the tower and correctly connecting the DC and AC wiring, as well as the batteries. If you don't have the appropriate experience and equipment to perform any of these things, then let the professionals do it for you. It's better than ruining an expensive system that is intended to serve you for many years ahead.

The system maintenance should be performed annually. And again, if you don't know how to perform these, a licensed and verified technician should be invited. The maintenance normally includes checking the parts for corrosion, checking the guy wires for required tension, tightening bolts and electrical connection and checking the blades. If necessary, blades and bearings are replaced once a decade. Also, the edge tape on the blades should be replaced once a year, if it's worn.

The Recommended Size

You know about the wind resource, the location, the system's part and the maintenance. But just how big of a system you should purchase? This depends on the kilowatt-hours that your house uses. Let's say that you use about 12,000 kilowatt-hour in a year. A wind turbine that produces 5 to 15 kW should significantly contribute to such a household.

Again, the manufacturer should be your number one source for all these calculations. There are several factors that affect the system's annual output, such as the tower's height, the turbine's power curve, the annual data of the wind speed as well as the number of hours that the wind blows during the year.

Finally, there is a formula that estimates just how big the system's annual energy output (AEO) can be.

$$AEO = 0.01328\ D2\ V3$$

D is the rotor's diameter in feet, and V is the wind's yearly average in miles per hour. The end result is in kilowatt-hour per year.

WATER SOURCES AND SANITATION

One of the first things you need to know when preparing to live off-grid is where, how, and how often you will get your water. A single person can go through 80-100 gallons of water a day, whether it be drinking, bathing, washing dishes, watering plants, or using the toilet. It all adds up.

You will use water for these reasons, and more:

- drinking
- bathing
- crop irrigation
- livestock
- medical emergencies
- dishes, laundry, cleaning

Therefore, you need to plan your water system before you plan anything else, like your garden and where you will put your livestock.

An important factor in deciding on your water sources is how you will use the water from those sources. For example, you might decide that the well water is for yourself, the rain water is for your livestock, and the stream water is for irrigating your crops (if you have a stream, that is).

Off Grid Water Sources

There are quite a few options when it comes to sourcing water for your off grid homestead. Take a look at the list below:

- City water: this is a perfectly viable option and

nothing to be ashamed of. People homestead at different levels of self-sufficiency, and sometimes city water is seriously the only option. That being said, it is a good idea to dig a little deeper (no pun intended).

- Rain water: this is an excellent source of water to *complement* the water source that you already have. It is possible to go weeks without rain, therefore, you should never depend on rain water as your primary source of water. That being said, it is incredibly wasteful to let the rain water run free.
  Some people invest in a rain water filtration or purification system (more information below) to make it safe to drink. Depending on where else you are sourcing your water, however, you may want to use rain water just for irrigation and your livestock.
- Wild water: water from a creek or stream. Flowing water is generally more filtered than sitting water.
- Well water: well water is almost always guaranteed to taste just a little bit different every time you fill up your bottle. Do not be alarmed. The weather, especially if you live near the coast, can influence the flavor of the water depending on what minerals are leached into the water from the surrounding land. As long as you regularly have your well water tested for harmful bacteria and the well water passes the test, it is safe to drink the water.
  While investing in a well is not cheap, it is, however, an incredibly reliable, essentially unlimited, and completely free source of water. Keep reading in the next section for more information on how to dig a well.
- Hauling water and storing it in a large tank: This is a great idea, especially if you have a wild water source nearby, for example, a lake or a stream. It might be possible for you to collect the water and store it in

the large tank. You might also consider the water haul and tank store option if you have access to a well that is a little ways down the street.

This list is by no means complete. That being said, the most successful off grid homesteads will have a well, and they will also source their water from more than one place.

Rainwater: Collecting and Storing

Depending on your desired scale, you can collect rainwater from your roof into a rain barrel, or you can install large cisterns to supply your entire household.

You should know how much rain you can collect in a year, which you can calculate with this formula:

1 inch rain x 1000 square feet = 623 gallons

Many people employ their roofs. The rain hits the roof and runs down to the gutters (which need to have a screening). The rain then goes through a downspout filter and a first flush diverter. These filters help remove contaminants. Before entering the tank, the water rushes through the tank screen, which keeps pests and mosquitoes out.

You can store your rainwater in a number of different types of vessels:

- Rain Barrels: a barrel is installed at the base of the gutter downspout. It is easy to install, readily accessible, and the barrels do not take up much space. However, they can easily overflow as capacity is normally at around 50-100 gallons.
- "Dry" System: this system has a larger storage capacity than the barrel, and the collection pipe dries after every rain. It can store a lot of rainwater, which is good for environments with infrequent rain falls. It is an inexpensive and simple system, but the tank must be located next to the house.
- "Wet" system: collection pipes are underground and

connect multiple downspouts from more than one gutter. The underground piping fills with water, overflows to the vertical pipes, then spills into the tank. Water-tight connections must exist in the underground collection piping and the downspouts, and the tank inlet's elevation must be lower than the lowest gutter. This system works well for large-scale collection, and can be located away from the house, but it is expensive and somewhat complex to install and maintain.

Wild Water: Installation of Water Pipes and Plumbing

Whenever possible, it is best to use gravity to your advantage, and to keep geographic proximity in mind. Here is how you can plumb wild water to your holding tank.

- **Step 1**: The sump hole should be right next to the water source. That way the water pools into the hole. Fill the bottom of the hole with rocks and a layer of sand.
- **Step 2**: Submersible pumps that push water are more effective than pumps that pull water, especially if the water is going uphill. You need to properly install your pump so that it is secure and not susceptible to sucking up the surrounding mud, sand, or other debris.
- **Step 3**: Connect your power source to the pump, remembering that electricity and water do not mix.
- **Step 4**: Route the water to your holding tank. A 500 foot run should have a pipe that is 2 inches in diameter. Any time the pipe needs to change direction, the angle should be no smaller than 90 degrees. Keep in mind the distance and elevation in creating your route.

Wells: Types, Permissions, Well Pumps

There are a couple different types of wells. Rest assured, there is probably one that will work for you.

Types of Wells

- **Dug wells**: How did people get their water before machinery? They dug deep holes in the ground by hand until water started seeping out from the rocks. When the incoming water was flowing faster than the hand-digger could dig, the digger stopped digging. While you can most certainly dig your own well, keep in mind that these are less safe than drilled wells. This is because they are shallower, making them more prone to contamination. In times of drought when the water table drops, the well might also run dry.
- **Driven wells**: A small pipe with a screen on the end is driven into soft ground until the pipe hits the water table. Like hand-dug wells, they are shallow, making them susceptible to contamination and running dry.
- **Drilled wells**: A combination of machinery, including drill bits, percussion bits, and auger bits, work together to drill a hole that can be more than 1,000 feet deep. The drill rig is mounted on a big truck, and is operated by a professional. Once the well is drilled, a pump is installed to bring the water up to the surface. This is your most expensive, but most reliable and responsible way to dig a well.

Permission to Dig a Well

You need permission to dig a well, which you can obtain by submitting an application to your county (if the area has plentiful groundwater) or state government (if groundwater is scarce). There will be an application fee of about $100-$150, and once your application is approved, you will get a permit.

The application will require certain information, and sometimes it is best for the well contractor to apply for the permit.

- Applicant/property owner information (name, address, contact information)
- Property address
- Parcel number/property ID
- Legal description
- Legal survey
- Well contractor (name and contact information)
- Proposed well information (size, depth, drilling method, casing type
- Site plan: see below.

Your site plan shows what is on your property and where the well is going to be dug. The well must be a minimum distance from the road, bodies of water, and septic systems.

You need to include:

- Proposed well
- What the well will serve
- Driveway
- Septic tank, drain field and system pipes
- Bodies of water
- Road(s)
- Scale of the site plan

Once you have your permit, you can start digging your well. There will be at least two inspections throughout the process, and the water will be tested at the end to ensure that it is safe to drink.

Powering your Well Pump

If you decide to drill your well, you must have some sort of power to fuel the pump that brings your water to the surface. Depending on the depth of your well, you have two choices: jet pumps and submersible pumps.

Jet pumps are for shallow wells. They are mounted above

the ground and suction the water from the well. Submersible pumps are popular for deep private wells. Like the name implies, they are installed inside the well casing and connect to a surface power source.

If you are routing water from a wild source, you will need to install a sump pump. A sump pump is a pump that is designed to remove water from a basin where the water has collected. Once you route your water to said basin, you will need a sump pump to move it to your home.

No matter the pump, however, try to use the abundant natural resources that are around you as a power source for your pump:

- Wind Powered Pump: great for flat terrain where wind is strong.
- Solar Powered Pump: if the sun stops shining, you are dead anyway.
- Hand Pump: the most budget friendly option is the hand pump. In fact, you can stay on your electric grid and use the hand pump as a backup in case of an emergency.

Once you have your well or sump basin established and your particular pump installed, you need to route the water to your home and everywhere else that you need the water to go.

No matter your methods of collecting and storing water, you need to know how to filter it into potable (drinkable) or non-potable (not drinkable) use.

Water Filtration and Purification Systems

It is important to filter your water, even if it looks clean. This is because harmful bacteria and pathogens, especially if the water came from a contaminated source, can kill you. You need to invest in a good off-grid water filtration system.

Consider the following when looking at a system:

- Type and level of treatment: must use filters and UV

radiation (not chemicals) to remove physical matter, contaminants, bacteria, viruses, and protozoa
- Powered vs Gravity Fed: gravity fed is not as fast as powered filters. Gravity can run independently of power, although though there are some viable options that run off of solar.
- Flow Rate: gravity will yield about 1-4 gallons per hour whereas powered will yield 1-4 gallons per minute. Figure out what you need.
- Water Storage Capacity: you want a system that is built to filter, not store.

There are simple DIY water filtration systems you can set up, however, these tend to be more unreliable.

- DIY Bio-Filters: filters, does not disinfect
- UV/Sunlight systems: does not filter, disinfects
- Ceramic: filters and disinfects
- Chemical: does not filter, disinfects
- Distillation: filters and disinfects
- Boiling: does not filter, disinfects

Greywater Sewage in Off Grid Living

Sanitation is a critical component of successfully living off grid. Without proper sanitation protocols in place, you are putting your health, and the health of others, at high risk. Runoff can be extremely dangerous if harmful pathogens and bacteria are present. Therefore, careful consideration and precautions must be taken. Luckily, there are laws that you must abide by, and the Environmental Agency must approve whatever system you have in place. As long as you are approved, you have nothing to worry about.

This being said, there are two types of water waste: greywater and blackwater. Greywater comes from sinks, washing machines, and showers. It can be processed and recycled, as it does not have the same harmful bacteria and pathogens that blackwater has. Blackwater comes from dishwashers and toilets. It needs to go back to the earth.

There are three stages to water treatment: separation of solids from liquids, biological filtration, and mechanical filtration. Biological filtration employs friendly bacteria that denature the harmful bacteria in a heavily oxygenated environment. Mechanical filtration filters the water, making it fully treated and ready for its return to the environment.

Living off grid means making things yourself and reusing things as much as possible. This is the case with water as well. Luckily, you can reuse greywater. If you are moving into an existing home, it might not be a practical decision to re-plumb. It is always wise to work within your means. Remember, one motive for off grid living is to lessen the impact on the environment. Can you make do with what you have?

You can easily recycle greywater by using it in toilets. All you need to do is filter it, apply the proper chemical dosage, then direct it to the toilet. There are greywater recycling products on the market that can do this. With more processing, you might be able to get it to meet the standards for the European Bathing Water Regulation 2006/7/EG, in which case you may be able to use it in showers, baths, washing machines, and even sinks.

If you are building your set-up yourself, definitely take greywater recycling into consideration. Up to 50% of your water can be recycled. That is a lot of water, a lot of money in your pocket, and a lot of relief on the global water supply.

Greywater Recycling Products

You can choose between a greywater diversion device and a greywater treatment system.

- The diversion device, like the Aqua2use Greywater Diversion Devices, recycles water from the shower, bathroom sinks, and washing machine. You can use this water for irrigation.

- The Matala filtration system also removes impurities, making the greywater safe for irrigation.
- The treatment system, like the Aqua2use Greywater Treatment System, has the same capabilities as the Aqua2use Greywater Diversion Device, and it also recycles, treats, and stores the water for use in the home.

If you have the right equipment, you can safely reuse greywater and simultaneously save money, conserve water, and be more environmentally friendly.

Blackwater Sewage in Off Grid Living

One of the reasons you should process your own waste is that it is better for the environment, and consequentially, healthier for you.

Here are the four most common options for dealing with your sewage:

- **Cesspool or cesspit**: This is a holding tank that stores the waste until a waste management company comes to pick it up. It has been banned in many countries as it is horrible for the environment. It requires a huge tank and leaves a very large carbon footprint.
- **Septic tank system**: This is a tank that separates the solids from the liquids. The liquid can then drain to a reed bed (see below for more information on the reed bed). When considering your options, you need to check with your local province or county to see if you can have a septic tank system.
- **Sewage treatment plant system**: A small-scale treatment facility, which produces fully treated effluent that is ready for release into the environment. This set-up is one of the best ways to get approval from the Environmental Agency, and to truly deal with your waste off grid.

- **Compost toilet and compost heap**: A self-containing system that takes care of itself. There will be more on this topic in the next section: Off Grid Sewage Options.

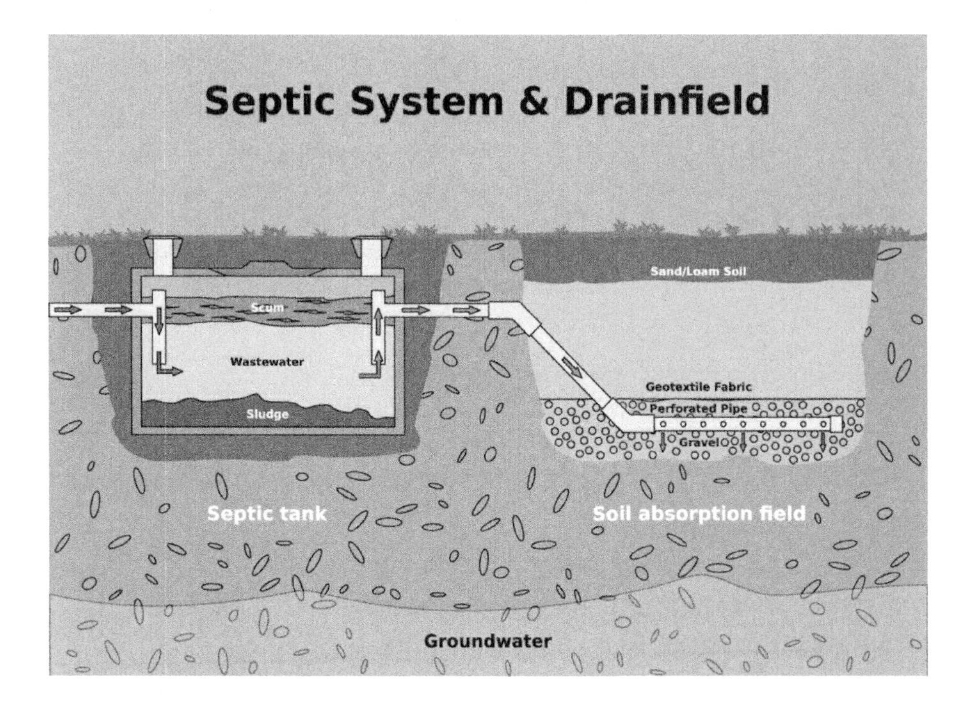

Septic Systems

Septic systems use a combination of proven technology and nature to treat household waste from kitchen drains, laundry, and bathrooms.

The septic system has two components:

- A septic tank: a buried, water-tight concrete, fiberglass, or poyethylene container that separates solids and floatable matter (grease, oil) and digests organic matter. The effluent is then discharged to the field. Pumps or gravity then move the effluent through sand, constructed wetlands, soil, or another medium to remove pathogens, nitrogen, and other contaminants. If it is soil-based, the waste enters perforated pipes that slowly release the waste into the ground.

- A drainfield: a covered, shallow excavation in unsaturated soil. The soil soaks, treats, then disperses the wastewater into the soil, which further filters it from harmful coliform bacteria (indicator of human fecal contamination), nutrients, and viruses. It then becomes groundwater.

You can install your septic system following these steps:

1. Prepare and design your system by doing a site survey and soil test.
2. Submit your application and wait for approval.
3. Dig the hole for the tank and route the pipe from the tank to the house.
4. Excavate the leach field.
5. Route the pipe to the leach field and surround it with gravel to keep the pipe in place.
6. After inspection, cover up the tank and pipe.

Your leach field can be a reed bed, which is an engineered pond of reeds that works with the natural ecological processes in order to break down the wastewater organic matter. The pond also consists of gravel and sand.

Wastewater settles at one end or across the entire surface. Since the atmosphere is rich in oxygen, the bacteria are able to effectively process the waste into treated effluent.

Composting Toilets

If you have not already begun to do so, you must consider installing a composting toilet. Composting toilets are already popular in tiny houses, RVs, boats, and off grid homesteads. They are safe, healthy for the environment, involve minimal effort, and can be very affordable. In fact, you can even make your own composting toilet, which oftentimes makes using the compost toilet much simpler than using one you would buy.

This being said, composting toilets are not legal in all places. You need to check with within your area to see if composting toilets are allowed, and if not, you need to learn about your next best option.

How Compost Toilets Work

Composting toilets are not attached to a septic or sewage system. They do not use any water, and they take care of themselves. There is no plumbing, chemicals, or flushing. They are organic and natural. So, what is the catch?

You must empty the bucket.

It is not that bad. The composting toilet does all the work for you, so emptying the bucket is like dumping out your coffee grounds.

Most composting toilets separate the solids from the liquid. This takes care of the smell. The solids fall to the back and the liquid is directed to the front. Most people empty the front tank every three days, and the back tank every three weeks. The liquids can be diluted with water and tossed onto land that you are NOT growing any food on. The solids can go in a compost bin that you are using for ornamental plants.

You do NOT want to put any human waste on any plants that you are growing for consumption. This is a recipe for disaster.

Types of Composting Toilets

Take a moment to learn about the different types of composting toilets.

- **Incinolet composting toilets**: These toilets essentially evaporate the fecal matter through the use of heat. These composting toilets require power, but the end result is dust which you can put in your non-food compost pile.
- **Self-sealing cartridge composting toilets**: This type of composting toilet seals the waste in plastic

bags, which you can then throw away. This system kind of defeats the purpose of having a composting toilet, however, because plastic is bad for the environment. Nevertheless, the set up might be easier for some people to deal with. These toilets are more affordable, but you will have to continue to buy plastic bags.

- **DIY composting toilet**: The DIY composting toilet is exactly as you want it to be. They are very affordable and easy to fix because you made it yourself. Below is a step-by-step guide for making your own compost toilet.

DIY Compost Toilet

This section is broken down into building the compost toilet, building the compost heap, and maintaining and using the compost heap.

Compost Toilet Supplies

- 20 liter bucket
- plywood
- toilet seat
- bin
- scoop
- sawdust

Compost Toilet Steps

1. Build a box big enough to fit the 20 liter bucket.
2. Place the toilet lid on top.
3. Do your thing (no need to separate the liquid from the solid).
4. Use the scoop to add the sawdust.

Compost Heap Supplies

- Two containers (each container should be 1.6 square meters, and 1.3 meters high.
- Straw or cardboard

- Designated turning fork

Compost Heap Process

1. Build the containers, then place a thick layer of straw or cardboard on the bottom.
2. Empty your bucket of waste onto the cardboard, then cover it with fresh straw or cardboard.

When you empty another bucket...

1. Use the designated turning fork to make a hole in the heap.
2. Empty the bucket into the hole.
3. Cover the fresh waste with the old waste, then cover the pile with fresh straw or cardboard.

Healthy Compost Heap Tips

- Keep the top of the heap flat.
- Add new material to the center of the pile.
- Include both liquid and solid waste to keep a balanced ratio of wet to dry ingredients.
- Keep the heap covered.
- Start the new heap in the second container when the first container is full.
- Only use the finished compost on plants that you are not going to eat.

The compost toilet is an excellent way to decrease your footprint on the planet in a safe and simple fashion. You must, however, use caution with your compost and compost heap. Never use the finished compost in or near your gardens or fields where you are growing your food.

A Helpful Reminder (Again)

Living off grid unfortunately does not mean you can do what you want when you want. You still live in a state, province, or county, and therefore, you must follow the law. If the law restricts you from digging a well, or if it bans the use of compost toilets, you either need to move to a new location, or you need to deal with it. You can always channel your creative energy into something else.

FARMING

Living off the grid does not usually require a lot of land. You work with what you have. Some may even argue that living off the grid is what we were born to do. It can be done where you are right now. When we go back to nature and survive off the land, we naturally acclimate to the seasons and the weather, and we intuitively know how to react to our own demands and those of the earth. The hardest part is making that first leap because there seems to be a lot to learn first.

You really cannot just plant a seed in the ground and expect to have tomatoes for months. That seed needs proper soil with great drainage, a reliable water source, and some TLC. This chapter is going to discuss what makes for good soil, how to achieve great soil with minimal weeds, how to irrigate your crops, how to grow fruits and vegetables, grains and herbs, how to store and preserve food, animal husbandry, and then of course the expected costs and anticipated workload. At the end, you will have a basic step-by-step of when, how, and even where to start living off grid.

Step 1: Soil Health

Before you do anything, you need to know what kind of soil you have. Without healthy soil, your plants suffer. Good soil will depend on what you want to grow. If you scoop up a bit of soil and have a sticky, malleable ball, then you have clay soil, which is very hard to work with. It is slow to drain and compacts easily, which means it requires a lot of aeration. If your soil feels and looks granular and crumbly, you have sandy soil. It is very permeable and has great aeration, but it will be dry, infertile, and leach water. If your soil is fluffy and forms a loose ball, you have loam, which is an equal proportion of sand, silt and clay. This soil is ideal because it has the benefits of water and nutrient retention, and proper drainage and aeration. Sandy loam is great for vegetable growing.

You can determine the type of soil you have by scooping about two inches of soil into a mason jar. Fill the rest of the jar with water. Add a teaspoon of dish detergent, which helps separate the different soil particles. Shake the jar, then let it rest for a day. The soil will separate, and you will be able to see the dominant characteristics of your soil based on how thick the different layers are.

Once you know your soil composition, you know whether or not you need to make adjustments in order to get that perfect crop yield. Regardless of the type of soil you have from the get-go, however, there are some basic good farming practices that you should incorporate into your lifestyle. Off-grid living is very demanding work, so you need to be smart about how you spend your time and energy. Work with Mother Nature and let her work for you.

Step 2: No-Till Gardening and Compost

The way you set up your garden will make or break your off grid experience. You want to save everything that the earth gives you, and put it back into the earth. No-till gardening is when you let old organic matter decompose on the ground to become the newest layer of topsoil. You then plant directly into this layer. By not tilling the soil, you are not disturbing the worms and microbes, which are hard at work. Any dormant weed seeds that are well below the surface will also stay well below the surface. While the first couple of years you may have a lot of weeds, the longer you practice a no-till gardening method, the more productive your garden will be at keeping weeds in check. This is because plant matter continues to break down, thus adding an additional layer of soil to the weed seeds that continue to get pushed further down.

When you let the organic material continue to settle, you are essentially composting. You can go one step further. Any food scraps, tree debris, egg shells, etc. can go directly into a compost pile. You want to keep an eye on your carbon and nitrogen ratios, as this will influence how fast your compost breaks down, and whether or not it will rot or dry out.

Animal manure is an excellent and critical component and ingredient for compost and off-grid living.

Step 3: Irrigation

Plants need water, and the last thing you want to do is water plants all day long. You can use the force of gravity to route water from a nearby stream, or you can go the more industrial route and set up irrigation drip-tape or overhead irrigation. It is best to work with the slope of the land, otherwise you may have to engineer a pump, which, though an option, is also a disaster waiting to happen.

Step 4: Growing Crops

Once you know your soil health and have a healthy farming practice like no-till, you can start planning your fruit and vegetable gardens.

How do you get started? First, look to see what grows well in your area. You can find out by asking other local growers, or looking in the history books to see what traditionally grew in years past. Then, decide what you like to eat. When first starting out, it is imperative that you grow what you like to eat. Otherwise, you will get discouraged. How annoying would it be if you invested a whole growing season and got only Swiss chard and beets, but you do not like Swiss chard and beets so you ended up buying kale at the grocery store?!

After you get the hang of it, and as your taste buds begin to acclimate to the fresh produce you are producing, you should start to experiment. Incorporate new foods into your crop rotation. Not only is this beneficial to your health, but it also keeps your soil balanced. Worse comes to worst, you can always sell it at the market or feed it to your livestock.

Herbs

Herbs are a must-have because they can spice up your typical foods to make a completely new dish. Not to mention, they are healthy, delicious, and easy to grow. It is a good idea to have a separate herb garden. You can make an herb spiral, which is a strategy for growing many different types of herbs in a little space. The herb spiral is essentially a pile of dirt, with stones that spiral down, thus making a little spiraling ramp. This set up creates many different environments:

- Dry environment (at the top, the water drains all the way down to the ground)
- Wet environment (at the bottom)
- Sunny side
- Shady side

Herb spirals should be strategically located right outside your kitchen so that you are inclined to grab some before cooking a meal. To build an herb spiral, create a pile of dirt about three feet high and six feet in diameter. Then, arrange rocks in a spiral from top to bottom. Let the herb spiral settle for a little while before planting anything in it so that any soil-settling or erosion will not absorb your herb seeds.

Fruits and Vegetables

Fruit and nut trees can take years to bear fruit, and therefore should be one of the first things that you plant. They will cast a lot of shade, so plan the location of your trees accordingly.

It is a great idea to set up a berry patch. Berries are perennial plants, which mean that they come back every year. They are great dried, frozen, preserved into jams, jellies and preserves, and eaten as is or in pies. Go crazy here, and you can even set up a you-pick garden, which would bring in extra income that might come in handy.

Vegetables can be broken up into different groups based on the nutrients that they need to survive. You have heavy feeders, light feeders, and heavy givers, and these groups need to be rotated so that your soil is never depleted. Your heavy feeders include crops like:

- asparagus
- beet
- broccoli
- corn
- strawberries
- okra

The heavy feeders should be followed by light feeders:

- carrots
- garlic
- leeks
- swiss chard
- sweet potato

Your light feeders should be followed by a heavy giver:

- alfalfa
- beans
- clover
- peas
- peanuts

A lot of times, your heavy givers can be cover crops. Cover crops are crops that cover the land, especially during the winter time, to not only draw depleted nutrients back into the soil, but help prevent soil erosion and compaction. Cover crops can be grown and harvested for livestock.

Grains

There are a lot of myths to debunk when it comes to growing grains. First of all, they are very easy to grow. Second, you do not need acres and acres. Third, you do not need any fancy equipment.

Once you have your grain seeds, plant them in a location with plenty of sun, about 6 inches into the ground. Use a seeder to get even distribution (this can look like a mason jar with holes poked in the lid. Once you have a harvestable crop, harvest it with pruning shears or a hedge trimmer (or something similar). Then, remove the seeds from the stalk by beating the stalks with a stick. Finally, you can remove the paper coating from the grain by pouring the grain from one bowl into another in front of a fan.

1000 feet of land will yield about one bushel of wheat, which is enough to make about 60 pounds of grain. I can make about 34 loaves of bread with that.

Step 5: Storing Crops and Saving Seeds

One of the most important parts of off grid living is crop storage and seed saving. It is unlikely that you will be able to eat all of your tomatoes during the summer, and that you will be able to grow more tomatoes during the winter. So, you can your tomatoes as sauce and salsas, and dry tomatoes into chips. When winter comes, you now have tomato sauce and paste for making soups and spaghetti dishes. You can add your dried tomatoes to salads, sandwiches and hummus recipes. There are many different ways to store your crops, but we will cover just a few, to include proper storage environments.

The proper storage environment is typically a cool, dark place in an airtight container. A wine cellar would work just fine, but if you do not have one (which is often the case) just be sure to keep them away from the oven and windows. A pantry would work equally as well.

Always label and date your preserved food.

Canning

There are two different ways to can: boiling pot method and pressure method. You can safely preserve tomatoes, fruits, jams, jellies, pickles and other preserves using the boiling pot but pressure canning is THE only safe way to can vegetables, meats, poultry and seafood.

There are precise recipes that you must follow in order to safely can all of your food. If you do not follow these instructions exactly, your food will spoil, or could make you very sick (possibly kill you). They are very easy to follow, and when done right, is a very rewarding and dependable way to preserve food for months (and sometimes years) to come. Ball has a gazillion recipes.

Freezing

You can freeze just about anything: fruit, vegetables, meat, seafood, and herbs. There are some recommended tips to follow when it comes to freezing vegetables first. Depending on the vegetable, you may want to skin or blanch before freezing.

Fermenting

Fermenting food is another way to preserve food. You can easily chop up a bunch of vegetables, add a little bit of salt and spices, and stick it in a fermenting crock. A couple weeks later, you will have fresh kimchi or sauerkraut. You can then preserve this by canning using one of the above canning methods. Again, there are specific recipes you can follow for making delicious fermented foods. They are also very healthy for you, as they provide loads of probiotics.

Drying

Drying is an excellent way of preserving food. You can dry in the sun, but it is helpful to have a food dehydrator. There are so many things you can dry: fruit (think fruit leather!) potatoes, beets, sweet potatoes, herbs, and meat. Many food dehydrators come with a recipe book that explains the appropriate temperature and drying time.

It is best to opt for a combination of different preserving methods, that way you are not surviving off of a bunch of canned green beans. Canned green beans are delicious, but so are beet and sweet potato chips.

Saving Seeds

The best way to save seeds is to watch them and dry them, then store them in a cool dark place in a sealed, dated, and labeled jar. Some seeds require stratification before planting again, in which case, you can freeze them. If you get in the habit of saving your seeds, not only are you saving money, but you are also truly depending on yourself for survival.

Raising Livestock

This might seem like a daunting task, especially if you are new to living off grid. Luckily, animals are pretty darn good at taking care of themselves, if given the proper environment. In fact, they can end up taking care of you and your garden, if you let them. Here is a list of livestock:

- chickens
- goats
- sheep
- pigs
- cows
- ducks
- horses
- turkeys

While it might be tempting to have ALL the livestock, it is a good idea to start small and with animals that you enjoy eating (yes, that might sound horrible). One of the beauties of living off grid is that you are not alone. We as human beings require human socialization. Find out what other farmers are raising near you. If there are plenty of local cattle ranchers, consider raising turkeys, sheep and pigs. Then you can work together and have a larger supply of meat.

It is very important to do thorough research on the personalities and needs of different animals. Goats, for instance, will eat anything in sight. Sheep, however, also provide delicious milk for cheese, are also edible, and do not eat everything in sight. Not to mention, you can get different breeds, some of which are better for their wool, milk, and meat.

Chickens are extremely easy to care for. Once they have a coop and a piece of land, they are set. They love to free range, and they will provide you with an egg a day. They need fresh water, a good and reliable source of calcium and protein, shelter (to include shade), and a place to take a dust bath. Chicken poop is an incredible crop fertilizer. You can even engineer a chicken tractor, which is a moveable enclosure that allows the chickens to graze exactly where you want them too. They poop on the land, and eat the bugs and the grass. When you move them along, you now have a perfect plot of land to grow in: no bugs, great fertilizer, and grass is all but gone.

Growing Feed for Livestock

It is a good idea to think about how you can feed your livestock from your own land. Animals do require certain nutrients, just like we do, in order to survive and be healthy. An easy way to have a dependable source of livestock feed is to grow cover crops during the winter, like rye, wheat, and oats.

A lot of people will grow extra vegetables just for their livestock. Animals love vegetables, and when it is time to butcher them, you know that they have eaten plenty of fruits and vegetables rather than grains, preservatives, and chemicals. Chickens love bugs and fresh greens, but pigs will eat canned vegetables.

If you have goats, save the brush from your lawn. Give your animals safe table scraps. Start a worm compost. Animals that free range will find sustenance from the land around them.

Anticipated Workload

The first couple of years will be hectic, difficult, and full of mistakes and failures. You will work hard, but remember that the work is seasonal. The spring and summer months will be busier than the fall and winter. Your harvest and food preserving weeks will be busier than your maintenance weeks. There will be a lot of physical labor and planning involved, but if you employ your animals, read and talk to others, have faith, and ask for help, the rewards far exceed the effort. You can only harvest what you seed.

CONTRACTING AND CONSULTATION

If you're truly serious about changing the way you live and start living off the grid, then one of the best things to do is consult with professionals who know every aspect of this world.

You have to be fully prepared when it comes to living off the grid. So, in order to fulfil all of yours and your family's needs and to be ready for any obstacle or surprise that may occur, getting advice and a detailed plan from professionals is the way to go.

In this chapter, I want to recommend about two such companies that can help you in any aspect of the off grid living, and also introduce you to a cool structure called OffGridBox, which is an all-in-one solution.

Off Grid Contracting

Off Grid Contracting is a service that specializes in private residential off grid construction and development. They serve the USA (but not only) on a variety of projects, from new construction to both small as well as large remodeling and renovation jobs. The company takes pride in meeting as well as exceeding any needs of their clients, thus making sure that the desired project is completed on time, on or below the set budget and that the clients are truly and 100% satisfied with the results.

What do they offer?

Off Grid Contracting offers different services, from consultation to construction services. Here are some of the services they offer, and you can also find pricings for each and every service on their website.

Full Service Consultation/Planning/Quote

- **Technical advice, consulting benchwork fee only**: If you prefer to construct on your own, yet looking for assistance.
- On-site inspections, on-site technical consulting.
- Blue prints, writing diagrams, site plans.
- Material resourcing, quote only on parts.

Construction services

- **Off grid real estate acquisition**: Helping you find a property that suits you and meets your expectation for both development and construction, and is also within your budget needs.
- **Container homes**: Helping design and construct a cargo container home that meets your requirements and specifications, including installation of off grid features.
- **Earth bag homes and hobbit homes**: Custom build of an of grid earthen home according to your desires and specifications.
- **Alternative energy**: Lower costs for materials and installation. This includes wind power, solar power, hydro power, thermal power, portable wheeled solar generators, solar power golf cart, utility cars, ATV, solar power for RVs, campers, travel trailers, vans, boats, and more.
- **Heating solutions**: Solar air heating (internal construction/exterior mount), solar water heaters, DC heating, wood stove installation.
- **Food production solutions**: Hydroponics/aquaponics and greenhousing.
- **Water solutions**: Rain collection systems, water filtration systems, DC/AC pumping options, atmospheric

water generator systems (water from air), pond aeration systems, hand pumps for wells.
- **Off grid security systems**: Remote and wired system, perimeter lighting.
- **Storm shelters/safe rooms**: Delivered to the location and installed, or built on the site of your location.
- **Service calls and maintenance**: Whenever you require them.

When considering such a job, it is important to understand warranty policies as well. Here are the two warranty policies and what they mean to you:

- **Parts warranty policy**: The warranty on all the parts that were provided and installed on the job location by Off Grid Contracting is provided by the manufacturers only. Parts that were bought by the customer and installed by the company are the customer's responsibility for those parts. However, Off Grid Contracting will help the customer in the process of warranty when possible.
- **Service warranty policy**: Off Grid Contracting currently offers a 90-day service labor warranty on all install work. However, it is important to know that this does not cover travel cost. If during the 90 days period there is any defect in the company's work, they will come out to service and fix the defects, provided they were caused by direct result of failure to properly install. The warranty also covers the company's work to replace any part that may have failed that is under manufacturer warranty. After the 90-day period, services will resort to the company's normal service call charges plus cost of travel.

For additional information and consultation, please visit Off Grid Contracting's site:

https://www.offgridcontracting.com

OffGridBox

The OffGridBox is a 6x6x6 feet container, fully equipped with everything needed in order to produce electricity as well as clean water. It is perfect for emergencies and natural disasters. Basically, it's a shelter to keep you warm and safe while providing clean drinking water.

The company is known for helping organizations and people all over the world, so it's not just for individuals. The OffGridBox is being used in villages worldwide to provide the people access to electricity and clean water. It also powers many electrical grids and serves as a disaster relief hub. Because the box is made of strong steel and the paint coating is durable, it can withstand a cyclone and stay fully operational even in extreme conditions and environments. The lifetime use of the box is 20 years!

The box can also be relocated, or you can resell it back to the company through their buyback program.

How does it work?

I mentioned that the box provides electricity and clean and filtered water. Here is how it works:

- **Energy**: The solar panel array on top of the box captures the energy of the sun, and then transforms it into direct current. This current is then converted by the inverter (that is already integrated) into electricity that you can instantly use. You can use this available energy right away for your home's needs, or store it in the batteries for later use. The battery is Lithium LiFePO 5.5 kWh with PAYG Add-On 17.5 kWh total or LeadGel (15kWh to 50kWh).
- **Water**: Collect water from any source you desire. It can be rainwater using the rain capture system that is already integrated with the box, or from other sources like lakes, rivers, wells, boreholes, and even oceans.

Then, store the water in the large polyethylene tank (600 liter internal tank) that is also integrated with the box in order to filter and clean the water. Some of the energy and electricity produced by the box is then used to clean, sterilize and filter the water, and then distribute the clean water whenever needed.

Add Ons

There are available Add Ons for the box. Their purpose is to increase production of energy, storage, and other features:

- Remote monitoring
- 300 USB ports
- Wi-Fi (32m range)
- Automatic irrigation
- Desalination of salt water
- Additional solar panels and storage of energy if needed

Dimensions

External Dimensions: L x W x H: 1.98m x 1.95m x 1.91m (6' 6" x 6' 5" x 6' 3")

Photovoltaic Array Dimensions: L x W: 4m x 5m (13.12' x 16.40')

Weight

Dry: 1,300 kg (2,866 lbs)

Wet: 2,800 kg (6,172 lbs)

Empty: 500 kg (1,102 lbs)

Certifications

CE certified

UL certified

What else?

- The box can be installed anywhere you want. All it requires is enough sunlight (as it generates power using solar panels on its roof) and stable soil to set it on.
- The box provides electricity (using solar panels), filtered and clean drinking water (collect water from

any source to filter it: rivers, wells, rainwater, lakes, boreholes), battery storage and Wi-Fi communication.

- The box is delivered by helicopter, boat or truck, anywhere in the world.
- The box is installed quickly and maintained easily no matter where you live.
- All the hardware fits inside the box, and modules are available for customization if needed.
- Installation of the box takes only 3 hours with basic tools.
- An estimate of 2 months from the time you purchase it to the box being fully operational.
- One unit of the box can serve up to 1,500 people.
- The box is friendly to the environment since it generates electricity using solar panels, as opposed to fuel or diesel.
- The box can be upgraded if required. You can add more solar panels, batteries and the company's water desalination system.

Applications of the box are extremely wide. It can provide electricity and water to schools, clinics and community centers, small farms and ranches, and of course to tiny homes, cabins and houses. As for the off grid living, this box is able to provide for a 2-bedroom household, depending on consumption habits.

For additional information and consultation, please visit the company's site:
https://www.offgridbox.com

Johnny Weiss Solar Consulting

Johnny Weiss offers professional services and consultation to both organizations and individuals. He has over 40 year of experience in the field, designing, reviewing and building solar, wind, and water power systems. He has been collaborating and consulting in over 30 different countries worldwide, including with Native American tribes.

How does he work?

Johnny Weiss works closely with the client in order to determine the viability of the project. Then, he will help assemble and design a team of professionals and list the necessary equipment for the project, bringing the solar dream and plan into reality.

Johnny is not just an expert when it comes to technical details, he is also great at solving problems, attacking them from a comprehensive point of view. He will gladly educate his clients with the required knowledge and skills for a successful solar project and be there with you all the way.

What does he offer?

As mentioned above, Johnny offers his services to both organizations and individuals. Here is what you get when you choose to collaborate with him:

Organizations:

- Renewable energy project management
- Developing solar training centers
- Training of trainers
- Renewable energy curriculum design and review
- Planning and design of hybrid renewable energy micro-grids
- Solar advocacy and speaking engagements

Individuals:

- Site evaluation for solar, wind and micro-hydro installations
- Plan review for residential and commercial solar projects
- Greenhouse design/build supervision
- Evaluation of off-grid energy alternatives

- End-user education

For additional information and consultation, please visit Johnny's site:

https://johnnyweiss-solar.com

OFF GRID COMMUNICATION

Living off the grid differs by far from living on the grid. By now, you probably know what living off the grid means, especially if you decide to live in a secluded area and away from cities.

You already know that you have to rely on yourself, grow your own food, supply your own energy power and basically get by all on your own. Often you will be far away from friends, family and immediate help.

This makes off grid communication vital for your survival. When there is no satellite communication, when the signal of the network is weak, when there are real emergencies, alternative off grid communication can be a real lifesaver.

So, preparing to live off the grid means also having reliable off grid communication devices that can work under any conditions, even the most extreme ones.

Also, off grid communication is extremely important when you participate in outdoor activities, such as hiking, camping, backpacking, and so forth. You want to have the ability to communicate no matter where you are, especially when there is no cell service available.

In this chapter, I will share with you some of the best off grid communication devices that work when mobile network is down, when there is no Wi-Fi signal, and even when there is no power.

Common Off Grid Communication Systems

Before I go over the special devices that work without the use of power or satellite signal, let's see how you can still communicate using the "ordinary" devices and systems.

Cell Phone

Today, almost anybody has their own private cell phone. Thanks to the highly advanced technology, cellphone coverage is available almost anywhere on the face of this planet. Almost. When your battery still has some juice and there is a signal, then you should have no problem to communicate by the cell phone.

First and foremost, try to have a cellphone with you even when you live off the grid. You can reach anyone using a cellphone. The variety of devices is enormous. All of them are usually small, convenient, easy to carry and affordable. When you need to make a call or send a text message, the cell phone should be your #1 choice.

Landline

Your second option, when it comes to both off grid and on grid communication, is having a landline. A landline may not be so popular these days, when everyone uses cell phones instead. Nonetheless, in an off grid situation, having a landline phone has its own advantages.

There can be times when your cell phone will not work or will not have a satellite signal. A landline gets its power from phone lines. This means that it will function and work even at the times when the main electric grid is down.

If a cellphone needs cell towers nearby in order to have a signal, a landline phone uses a different technology. It's less complicated and is not prone to congestion, unlike those cell phone towers.

Satellite Phone

Another option for off grid communication is having a satellite phone, which is an extremely reliable form of communication. These phones don't make any use of cell towers, and instead connect to the satellites orbiting above the Earth.

A satellite's orbit can be high, medium or low. According to NASA, some communication satellites have high Earth orbit, while those in medium Earth orbit are designed more for navigation purposes and mostly monitor a specific area and region. Low Earth orbit satellites are used for scientific purposes.

Using those satellites for communication requires a subscription plan. Phones from companies such as Globalstar, Iridium and Thuraya are connected to satellites of low Earth orbit. Immasat phones are connected to satellites of high Earth orbit. My tip to you is to always check the regions and countries that are covered by the network before you sign up to a plan.

The satellite phones allow you to do pretty much what a cell phone does. You can make calls, send text messages, and even get online and access the global Internet.

Satellite phones work on a model of subscription. They are often utilized during hikes to remote places and outdoor activities, where there may not be any cell phone signal. There are models of satellite phones that allow you to use them on a daily basis. This means paying some kind of monthly fee or a single-time fee, which allows you to send an SMS message.

Satellite phones may be a bit costly, but they serve as a terrific backup system for off grid communication.

Here are some recommended satellite phones:

Iridium Extreme 9575: The phone allows you to make calls and receive them, send and receive SMS messages, track position using GPS, and use an emergency SOS button to request for help from anywhere in the world. It meets the standards of U.S. military. It's extremely durable as well as resistant to shock, dust, blowing rain, vibration, and more.

Inmarsat IsatPhone 2.1: Just like the Iridium Extreme 9575, this phone lets you make and receive calls, send messages and track your location using GPS. Resistant to dust, water (including jets of water), shock, dirt, and other hazards. It comes with probably one of the best batteries on any satellite phone. This means 8 hours of talk and 160 hours of standby.

Advanced Off Grid Communication Systems

And now it's time to go over the more interesting and advanced off grid communication systems, those that work where regular systems fail. Most of the devices here are used and designed for outdoor activities and ventures, but can serve you throughout your off grid living as well.

goTenna Mesh

When you find yourself in a place where there is no Wi-Fi, power or mobile network, goTenna Mesh is a great communication option and device. You can use it during emergencies, natural disasters, while off the grid living in remote places, or during such activities as fishing, hiking, climbing, and so on.

The goTenna Mesh is first paired with your own cellphone device through Bluetooth, and then it allows you to communicate with other users of up to 4 miles. Neither Wi-Fi nor cell service are required. A lot of adventurers use this device to keep in touch when travelling in groups to places with weak or no cell signal.

Using the goTenna Mesh, you are also able to:

- Share GPS locations
- Communicate during emergency situations
- Create group chats
- Download maps (free and offline)
- Share your whereabouts and location

- Send messages (private messaging, too)
- Emergency beacon (an emergency message that you can program)
- Encrypted private chats
- goTenna Plus (app that allows you to transmit a message using a nearby user, who has a cell service, to anyone else)
- Battery can last for 24 hours

Spot 3 Satellite GPS Messenger

When you find yourself in an emergency situation, the Spot 3 Satellite GPS Messenger lets you send an S.O.S. using your location via GPS, allowing search and rescue teams to know your exact spot.

The Check-In feature is a message that you can program ahead and let your friends and family know that you are okay and safe.

You can also send and save the location, which allows the contacts to track your progress with the use of Google Maps.

Garmin inReach Explorer+

The Garmin inReach Explorer+ uses 100% global Iridium coverage. This lets you message, track and use interactive SOS anywhere on the globe. The interactive SOS is a 24/7 search and rescue center that helps any time you find yourself in emergencies and life-threatening situations. You can also track as well as share your location to notify friends and family where you're at.

Download maps, aerial imagery in color, U.S. NOAA charts, and more by using a free-of-charge Earthmate app. You can exchange messages with any cellphone as well as contact email addresses from anywhere on the globe. When you use the interactive SOS service, you can even get a confirmation when help and rescue are on their way to you.

Spot X 2-Way Satellite Messenger

The Spot X, like the other devices is also a great device for emergency situations. It lets you exchange messages with cellphones and emails no matter where you are in the world. Send an S.O.S. distress signal to the search and rescue center that works 24/7, and receive a message when help is on your way.

Your friends and family can follow your progress using Google Maps, and you can share your tracking activity with them.

The Check-In feature can let everyone know you're safe and okay. You can even post a link to various social accounts, which is also a way to update your close friends and family about your progress and condition.

Radacat Team Messenger

This is a radio communication device that knows how to pair with your cellphone via Bluetooth. It's excellent to have on you, when you engage in outdoor activities such as hiking, cycling, skiing, and more. This device can be a lifesaver in cases of emergencies and even during international travels.

Even when the cell signal or service is down or unavailable, you can still operate the Radacat for all your needs. Use the GPS offline, send messages (both text and voice), and share your location in real time with other users.

By creating a private network, you can communicate and use GPS tracking even when there is no cell signal. There's no need in any fee, no weekly fee, no monthly fee, no need for Wi-Fi, cell or satellite services.

Here are some more great features of this device:

- Create private chat groups
- Send messages using an app, or send automatically using the shake-to-talk feature
- Mesh networking is long range. Peer-to-peer can reach

a range of up to 4 miles, or even more when you're in open spaces and environments.

- Download HD quality maps from anywhere in the world to prepare for your next trip, and use the maps offline.
- The battery can work and last for up to 36 hours.

Beartooth Walkie-Talkie

The Beartooth Walkie-Talkie is a device that works with your cellphone. It lets you make calls, send messages, use maps and share location with other Beartooth users, among other things. All these features are available to you, even though there is no cell service.

So, how does it work? A localized network is created between users in a specific range of one another. Whenever one of the users begins to talk, sends a message or shares his location in the app, this data is transferred through the created network.

Here are more features of the device:

- It is small and comfortable to carry and handle
- The device can be used as a backup battery for your cellphone
- The networks are independent and don't need any cell signal or Wi-Fi to operate
- The device operates in the ranges of 902-928 MHz

Gotoky

Another great option for off grid communication is the Gotoky (a Kickstarter project). It works on a mesh network, allowing you to make calls, text, navigate, activate emergency location beacon to call for help, and generally stay connected. All of this is made possible even when coverage of network is unavailable.

The group chats, which include both calls and texts, are secured. But wait, there is more. Need to navigate your way? No problem. You get access to offline topographic maps, share locations, live tracking, create events, etc.

So, how does the Gotoky work? The Gotoky is paired with the cellphone through Bluetooth. When the two are paired, it can connect to another Gotoky device, even if it's miles away, thus allowing the two devices to communicate.

Another great feature of this device is that you can double the range when creating your own network. The range can also be extended by other users. This means that in cities, valleys and forests the range can be extended up to 1.6 km/1 mile. In mountains, sea and open fields the range can be extended up to 8 km. In high buildings and mountain tops the range can be extended up to 30 km.

Additionally, it offers:

- Private chats (1-on-1 as well as groups)
- Record voice messages
- Hands free speaking
- Location pinging
- Route recording
- Share your GPS coordinates
- Compass
- Store up to 1,000 messages on the device without connecting to the cellphone
- Integrated antenna, so it won't break
- Works on 868 MHz as well as on 915 MHZ frequencies
- Resistant to dust and water
- 1 Watt of output power for high-powered transmissions
- Battery can last for up to 72 hours

Fogo

Fogo (another Kickstarter project) is so much more than just a device to communicate off the grid. It combines a walkie-talkie, GPS and flashlight, and can serve as a backup battery.

The device is built to answer the needs of the outdoors. You can carry your cellphone in the backpack and keep it safe. Communicate outdoors? Just use the Fogo. Use it as a walkie-talkie to talk to other users. Hiking? Use it for activity tracking and get stats of speed, elevation, distance, time, and more. Plus, you can share your location and even use this device as a flashlight in dark places.

The Fogo does not need any cell service or Wi-Fi in order to work. It can operate in a radial range of 16 miles when conditions are good, and 7 miles when weather conditions are bad or challenging.

Here are a few more great features of this device:

- Powerful flashlight (1200 lumen)
- Waterproof and durable
- Can work in extremely harsh conditions (above 35 degrees Celsius and below freezing temperature)
- The device and its software are especially designed for communication and navigation off the grid
- The battery can last for weeks and even months (depending on the use)
- Can charge your cellphone's battery

The only drawback of this device is that it communicates through peer-to-peer, and it's not supported by mesh network.

Ham Radio

The ham radio is ideal for off grid living, but not for outdoor activities like the devices I've just mentioned above. It costs less than the previous devices, and can be a crucial lifesaver during emergencies and disasters.

It takes some time to get to know to operate the device

quickly (which is important especially during emergency situations), and it needs to be connected to a power supply. However, the ham radio is cheaper than the other devices and very reliable for off grid communication.

The ham radio is mainly for those who:

- Live off the grid
- Live in remote locations
- Live alone
- Live in areas that are prone to natural disasters (tornadoes, earthquakes, hurricanes)

OFF GRID INTERNET

Deciding that you are going off the grid does not entail completely removing yourself from the civilized world. Yes, the off-grid life is a green, healthy, more independent lifestyle, but it does not mean that you revert to barbarism. You can still fully enjoy an access to the Internet and to the wealth of information, people and services it provides. Off grid Internet is real and entirely achievable, even if you reside in a remote region of your country.

Let's go into detail and see how you can get online while living off the grid.

5 Ways to Obtain The Off Grid Internet

1. Cell Phone

Cell phone Internet is an obvious and common choice. Cell towers exist even in the most remote off the grid areas, providing easy access to the Web. Any cell phone in your possession will get you the Internet access. This is probably the cheapest way of all those mentioned in this chapter. Although the phone screen is small and its abilities can be limited (as compared to a laptop), you can still freely use it to browse websites, send instant messages and read emails.

A cell phone connection has tons of advantages, such as:

- It's entirely mobile, you can carry your phone and the Internet access to any location.
- If your phone model allows this, you can activate the tethering/hotspot option and distribute the off grid Internet to other nearby devices.

- Low costs, as compared to anything else on the list.
- Naturally, you can also use it for calls made from and to your personal phone number.

While this sounds ideal, there are a few caveats. First, you must ensure that the carrier of your choice covers your location. For that, you need to check their coverage maps. If you live in the United States, then you know that there are four main phone carriers. Here are the links to their maps:

- Sprint
- AT&T
- Verizon
- T-Mobile

Enter your address or zoom in on your location, and you will get the idea just how strong their signal near you is. In some areas, this info might not be 100% exact or up-to-date, but at least you can be sure that a phone carrier covers your off grid homestead.

Another way to find out is to ask anyone who lives nearby, or to borrow a phone that's already connected to one of the cell phone carriers. Walk across your lot and around its perimeter. Notice the strength of the signal and the Internet speed, and decide whether they seem satisfactory to you. You can use an online Speed Test or install their app for precise testing.

Now let's have a few words about **unlimited plans**. This term mostly refers to the total time of your phone calls. However, the providers usually don't let you use an infinite number of gigabytes of Internet data. Your actual data limit ranges from 20 to 50 GB a month. Once you cross this limit, your connection can be deprioritized, which translates to lower Internet speed. This is, of course, not a strict rule; it's just something that might happen if the local network is overloaded.

By "local network" I mean the total number of Internet connections in your vicinity. If you live in a city and you have reached the limit of your monthly data plan, the busy network will decide that you don't deserve the full speed. On the other hand, off-gridders who live in less populated areas have shared that they never felt deprioritized, even when they passed the 50 GB limit.

Living in a rural area has a certain disadvantage, too. A long distance from the closest cell tower negatively affects the quality of your off grid Internet connection. What you need in this case is a **cell phone booster**, which will amplify the weak signal and improve the connection in your area. A booster will cost you between $100 and $1000, but it's a one-time payment, and it's well worth the investment.

A cell phone booster overcomes the remoteness of your off-grid homestead. As I said earlier, establishing your own home does not mean cutting ties with the modern world. So don't let the distance force you to live with a weak signal. A cell phone booster is very simple to use, you just set it up and enjoy phone calls and online data, no matter how far you are from a cell tower. It works in any weather, unlike some of the satellite modems. If you own a smartphone and a boosted 3G/4G/5G signal, then you can have the best off grid Internet access possible.

A typical cell phone booster usually has 3 parts:

- **External antenna** that usually sits on your roof or on a pole outside the house. Find out where exactly the nearest cell tower is and direct the antenna towards it, to pull in the signal.
- **Signal booster** itself, which connects to the external antenna by cable. It amplifies the signal received from the antenna. A much stronger signal is then transferred to the inner antenna.
- **Inner antenna** is placed indoors, preferably mounted in the center of your homestead. It distributes the signal throughout the house and to your cell phone.

2. Private Hotspot

This is probably one of the most dependable ways to stay online. It does require some initial investment, but it lets you have many devices plugged into the same Wi-Fi hotspot. The devices' Internet connection will probably be much faster than anything provided with a mobile phone plan.

To establish your own Wi-Fi hotspot, you will need wireless provider that guarantees to supply online access around the clock. There are several companies today, cell phone carriers included, that provide you with a wireless Internet. You can use this Internet to work from your tablet or personal computer while you live off the grid.

In addition, you can also use a signal amplifier and a Wi-Fi antenna, to cover your entire homestead with an off grid Internet access.

3. Satellite

This method for off grid Internet solves the problem of large distance from any hotspot or cell tower. Satellite Internet helps even the most remote homesteads to stay connected. Companies like WildBlue, HughesNet, DISH Network and a few more provide affordable high-speed Internet connection via satellite. Some of them even provide satellite television as a part of the same bundle.

For example, HughesNet has monthly plans of up to 50 GB per month, plus additional 50 GB when you use the Internet during the night hours. Plus, they include the innovative **Gen5 system**, which is considered the best satellite service today. This system guarantees 3 MBPS upload and 25 MBPS download speeds, so you can freely stream music and movies whenever you like.

HughesNet modem also comes with a Wi-Fi option, for all your electronic devices that need an Internet access. You can control your data usage from their mobile app. Furthermore, you can control the “data saver” feature that dictates how you view videos. This helps using less data while you view more movies and videos.

While the satellite Internet is a great solution for your off grid Internet needs, there are a few cons that you need to be aware of. The satellite Internet speed can be somewhat affected by peak hours and weather. If the sky is not clear, the connection’s quality might be reduced. Additionally, satellite Internet might not be the ideal way if you need to stream or use a service like WhatsApp call or Skype – there can be some lag, unless you use the aforementioned Gen5 system.

Another issue is the satellite modem. While it’s necessary to receive the satellite Internet, it can be power-consuming. I would advise to turn it off when you don’t need the Internet, otherwise will consume up to 30W of your power resources.

At this point I should also mention **RV satellite systems**. Many people, who live off the grid, actually live in a motorhome or an RV. They change locations, which makes the Internet access much more challenging. Fortunately for them, some companies provide satellite Internet for the boondockers, ensuring that they stay connected even while travelling and parking in the most distant regions of the country.

I must warn you, however, that the investment into an RV satellite system is costly. You will need to permanently mount this system on your roof, and the total cost can be about $2,000. On the bright side, you now have a reliable system that will pull in a satellite connection, no matter where you currently are.

4. Ham radio

This might surprise some of you, but a ham radio can also get you an off grid Internet access. Once you establish a repeater network, you can use ham radio to have an online connection. It won’t be strong enough for video streaming or file downloading. However, it lets you send important data, such as documents and emails. This can be an excellent solution in an extreme scenario, when other means of communication fall.

Once upon a time, when the luxury of the global Internet was still far away in the future, ham radio had an Internet-like network of its own. It's called Packet Radio. Packet Radio was very useful when you needed to send texts and files, control devices and systems, post on bulletin boards, and so forth. If the worst happens and the Internet disappears, this ham radio-based technology can still serve as an emergency online web.

These days, we have such global messaging systems as Winlink, DStar and some others. People who operate a ham radio can use them to relay important messages, communicate in a case of emergency, send emails with attached files, and actually browse the Worldwide Web. It's not an ideal solution, as you would probably not want to broadcast personal passwords or some other sensitive data via the radio Internet. Nonetheless, once a doomsday scenario happens, beggars can't be choosers. The ham radio Internet will suffice.

To summarize, a ham radio is a really affordable solution that works when anything else fails. If you had worked with ham radios in the past, then you can easily get the Internet through them. The radio Internet has its limitation, of course. It's not as fast as you'd probably want it to be. The access is not secure, and the sent data can be listened to by anyone else who uses your frequency. You also need a nearby ham radio or a repeater station to operate yours and get online.

5. Unlimitedville

Unlimitedville is a unique approach to off grid Internet providing. If you are a member of Unlimitedville, then you can enjoy a truly unlimited data. This wireless access does not come directly from the big 4 American providers. Instead, Unlimitedville lets its members use this organization's hotspots and Internet routers.

Keep in mind that the plans offered by the large carriers are not exactly uncapped and unlimited. Usually these companies limit hotspots and tethering to 10 GB/month at most. This is done to force more people to subscribe to their services.

On the other hand, Unlimitedville is not greedy. It functions as a big community that always welcomes new members. Unlimitedville makes sure you always have a fast and steady Internet connection. They provide limitless W-Fi to any device that you have in your off the grid home. That means your phone, computer, TV, and anything else that works with the off grid Internet.

Their Internet speed varies based on your distance from a cell tower. The more remote areas get about 1 MBPS, while folks who are closer to a tower report speed of at least 70 MBPS.

Unlimitedville is also much closer to the off-grid spirit, as it does not demand signing any contract. You pay on a monthly basis, no checks needed. If you decide to cancel the membership, you just return their hotspot and that's it.

If you're still hesitant, they have a 14 day money back guarantee. You do not risk anything, as you can return the hotspot and get a full refund. By the way, I am not by any means associated with Unlimitedville. I simply suggest this service as another way to get an off grid Internet access.

PART 4: MOBILE AND URBAN OFF GRID LIVING

WHAT IS A SELF-CONTAINED RV?

As you understand by now, living off the grid is quite often living in a rural, remote area. But other off-grid setups are available as well. You can live off the grid in a vehicle or even in a city. Let take a look at these interesting options.

It's quite possible to live off the grid in an RV (recreational vehicle). But first, let's discuss RVs in general, especially the so-called self-contained RVs.

Basically, self-contained RVs have all the essential additions that makes you independent of whatever the campsite offers. Usually it contains a generator, sewer tanks and running water. Most of the American RVs are self-contained, and they make your trip much easier and more enjoyable.

Most – but not all of them. A class B motorhome is not always self-contained. But I am getting ahead of myself. There are many RV-related questions that must be answered in depth, before you make your choice of purchase or rental. For instance, what's the level of self-containment that any RV can have? How long can you use it for, without requiring any electric hookups or outside utilities? What exactly are the different motorhome classes, and which one is the best for you? What driver's license do you need for an RV? And so on.

Let's try answering these and other questions, shall we?

Self-Contained RV – Definition and Classes

You could be on the road for a holiday or vacation, or

you could be living off the grid. Either way, a motorhome or campervan has always been America's favorite choice of such a travel. You drive and live in an RV without fully relying on any external resources. A good RV, as I just mentioned, has a toilet as well as a container for graywater from the shower and the sink and for septic waste. Which means you can just park for the night without searching for public restrooms. And then you're simply gone in the morning, driving off with all the essential facilities within the RV.

There are several RV variations available, but basically there are two main types – towable and motorized. The motorized ones are the main subject of this chapter, they are usually self-contained, and one can drive and live in them. I have a prepared a table of three major motorized RV classes for your convenience:

Class	Class A	Class B	Class C
Size	21-45 feet	17-19 feet	20-31 feet
People	1-8	1-4	1-8
Facilities	Fully equipped with all the essentials and luxuries, making it a literal home on wheels.	It has a limited living space and does not always come with fresh water and toilet. On the other hand, it comes with cooking equipment, a fridge, a heater and beds.	Similarly to Class A, it has the cooking amenities, heating, AC, entertainment equipment, and so forth. The sleeping quarters are usually above the cab, plus there is another one in a slide-out addition at the back.
Notes	The biggest class, and also the most expensive one.	The smallest of all classes, lower price, easier operation, very adaptable.	This is a smaller version of Class A. It's actually a campervan, not a motorhome.

With this table in mind, ask yourself these three crucial questions before deciding on the best RV class for you:

1. How many people will be traveling in the RV – there-

fore, how many beds it should have?

2. What is your travelling plan? Will you be staying at the same spot for several days, or do you plan to move a lot and visit many different landmarks?
3. How much money do you intend to spend? Your budget should include such expenses as gas and insurance.

If you can answer these, then choosing an RV class becomes an easier task. I will add more information below that can help you to come up with a definite answer. Let's proceed and understand even further what it means to have an RV.

Why a Self-Contained RV Is the Best Choice for You

Again, a Self-Contained RV is something that you can use and drive without needing any external sources. When you camp it, you don't need to worry whether or not the site has any hookups. This is what we call a "boondocking" or "dry camping": you park anywhere without hooking your RV to the local power grid, water grid or sewage. You have everything that you need in the RV, and that is where it all stays as well.

For the perfect boondocking experience, your RV must be equipped with the following systems:

- A big water tank for all your washing and showering.
- Big gray water and black water tanks that contain your used water and waste.
- A complete electrical system, powered by either a generator or by big batteries.

What to do if you don't have these? Well, then you're not self-contained and can't dry camp. You would need to find a campsite with a power grid you can connect to, as well as a hookup for water and an access to the sewage, to dump the waste. Furthermore, the campsite would need to have showers and public WC. Good luck stumbling there in the dark and using the same space used by hundreds before you.

Please notice that you would need, from time to time, to find a campsite or any other locations that has a dumping station. This is where you get rid of the accumulated waste and gray water. Never dump these anywhere else, the last thing we want is a negative environmental impact! This is another reason why a non-contained RV is inferior to a self-contained one – it has no means of containing the waste, which is often dumped in the most inappropriate places.

More on RV's Water and Sewage

Speaking of water hookups and dumping stations: how long until you will need these? Well, the deciding factors are the frequency of your bathroom and water usage, as well as your tanks' volume.

Usually, a typical self-contained vehicle can contain 3 days of waste until you'll need to stop by a dumping station. As I said earlier, you can find these near most of the campgrounds. Searching online for one is always a good strategy.

If you wish to remain off the grid for a much longer period of time, consider investing in much bigger tanks. Try saving water as you do so, and enjoy your stay away from the hookups and dumping stations.

The RV's Electric Setup - Batteries and Generator

And what about the electricity, how long will it take before you'll need an electric hookup? First of all, your RV has batteries, but these can be somewhat limited. Any large appliances that you might have, including your AC system – the batteries won't be able to power them.

Therefore, you will also need a fuel-powered generator. The generator will influence how long you can travel without needing an electric hookup. There are many models of generators available for purchase. The portable ones can run between 8 to 20 hours. A built-in generator can operate even longer, for days, providing that you look after it.

Types of Campsites

Campsites can be free or paid. There are two major distinctions between paid campsites that are relevant to any RVer. There is a powered camping site and a non-powered one. The powered campsites have all the hookups, you can get all the electricity that you need and plug appliances and electronics in. These sites cost more than their non-powered counterparts, so you can add that as another expense to cover, if your RV is not self-contained.

So if you're driving a self-contained vehicle, its own power grid allows you to park at the non-powered locations and save a buck or two. Yes, you don't have to park in the middle of nowhere, you can boondock on a camping site, not too far from the urban area. Or even choose a free spot inside a city – see the options below.

Best Free Parking Spaces for an RV

There are free camping areas, which can be ideal for a self-contained RV. The so called "freedom camping" can be anything from a simple dirt lot to fully equipped, albeit rare, camping sites with all the luxuries. Freedom camping has various conditions and laws, and they are not the same in every country or state, so you better research them online well ahead. Nonetheless, some of us use the freedom parking to live off the grid in an RV.

Personally, I'd recommend use both freedom camping and the paid one. You'd need a paid campsite about once in 3 days to charge the batteries and dump the waste and gray water tanks.

If you're searching for free camping spaces for your RV, I'd look for these in your vicinity:

- **Rest areas**: you can park there for free, but make sure you know the local laws, as it might not be legal in some states. Truck drivers also use these to park for the night, so check for available space in advance.

- **Walmart**: these stores usually have enormous parking lots, where you can stay for the night for free. But the policy may vary from store to store, so check with the manager first. You can also look online for a feedback from other RV enthusiasts who parked there.
- **Truck stops**: they have parking areas allotted specifically for recreational vehicles. Check ahead if they are free, because it's not always the case. Again, search online for reviews of a stop you're interested in, it may not always be very hospitable.
- **Repair shops**: this one is a twofer, as you can fix something that you planned to fix for a while, and also spend the night. Usually a car repair shop wouldn't mind to have you as the last customer in the afternoon, or a very first customer in the morning, and you can stay before or after the fixing is done.
- **Churches, temples and other holy places**: they mostly have large parking spaces, although these can fill according to whatever day is celebrated the most. For instance, a church's parking area will be full on every Sunday.
- **Casinos**: a large volume of American and Canadian casinos encourage to park nearby, to attract customers and players. If you have ever been to Vegas, you'd notice that the parking spaces resemble actual campsites, with all the RVs parked nearby. There are no hookups, and the lots are crowded on holidays and weekends, but you'll probably find a space to fit in.
- **Schools**: you will need a permission to park next to a school. They usually have wide parking spaces for the local community. Their advantage is that nobody uses them on weekends. Just make sure you'll be gone very

early in the morning, before the school starts.

Let's Talk About RV Prices

Campervans and motorhomes have a distinctive gap in rental price, which you will see right away. It's less costly to rent a minivan that was converted into an RV than a luxury unit that can fit several people. However, even if the rentals prices for the self-contained RVs are somewhat higher, you save tons of money along the way. As I explained above, you can use free campsites instead of paying for hookups and campsite utilities. Think about the long run, of all the time and money saved by a self-contained unit, and you will see how the price gap narrows in your favor.

If you intend to buy a self-contained RV, the price range is amazingly wide. You can get a used trailer (whose condition is still good) for as low as $15,000. On the other hand, you have luxury units and 5th wheels, whose price can go up and above $100,000. These are also the costs of living completely off the grid.

This is where you have to decide how much you want in your RV versus how much you can spend. The most basic self-contained unit should have a toilet with a water supply and waste tank. This setup will, of course, cost the least. Should you desire more amenities and luxuries, the prices will naturally rise. However, you will create a feeling of a real home. If you intend to travel a lot, especially with a family, adding more features is well worth the price bump.

So seriously consider creating a true home feeling in your vehicle. There are excellent and fully equipped RVs available that contain complete kitchen, several areas for different purposes (lounge, dining area, bedrooms) and of course a personal shower. They also have all the top notch appliances, such as fridges, water heaters, microwaves, ovens and even awnings, among many others.

There is one expense that you cannot avoid, and we all have to be aware of it when we allocate a budget for an RV. The gas mileage. You will need more gas for an RV, and the prices in North America tend to rise during the summer. Of course there are efficient ways to deal with it. Research and the plan your journey through the gas stations with the lowest prices. They are usually situated along the smaller roads, while those along the highways are usually the ones with the highest gas prices.

You can, of course, somewhat reduce your gas consumption and cut down the costs. For instance, main a good tire pressure, make sure your rubber is in top condition. Drive steadily, as sudden accelerations spend more gas. Also consider packing less and remove unnecessary weight. A lighter RV needs less fuel. Routinely check your engine to ensure that it functions efficiently. Periodically visit a mechanic to replace oil, air filters and anything else that can improve the mileage. These and similar strategies can reduce your expenses, so that you can enjoy your travel without worrying too much about the costs.

What Driver's License Do You Need to Drive an RV?

The quick answer is that most of the RV classes require just a regular license to drive. However, several US states demand a separate license issued specifically for driving a large RV. The rules are different for various states. Here are some examples:

- **Wisconsin**: if you have a commercial driver's license, be aware that its manual says that you can drive a five-wheeled motorhome, as long as it does not exceed 45 ft. in length.
- **Hawaii**: if your motorized home is somewhere between 15,000 lb. and 26,000 lb., you need a class 4 license. Anything heavier than that requires a commercial driver's license.
- **Connecticut**: here they have a unique variation for trailers over 10,000 lb., called a class 2 license.

So as you can see, always check ahead if you have the appropriate license for the RV of your choice.

Please notice that a motorhome can be a challenging vehicle. Driving a large house of wheels with all the amenities requires some skilled maneuvering. Not only will you be driving unfamiliar roads, you will also need sometimes to make your way through a city in this large vehicle. Parking an RV also demands some experience. Perhaps take your new motorhome for a short journey at first, just to get a feel of it.

OFF THE GRID RV LIVING

While RV living is primarily associated with those people who have retired or have saved money to be able to travel, it is important to note that there is also a large group of families and individuals, who sold their homes and now live in off grid vehicles. As a matter of fact, approximately one million Americans are currently exploring the RV living.

Choosing the RV lifestyle comes with a plethora of adventures, but jumping straight into off the grid RV living also brings a myriad of questions. Can an RV serve me as a complete house? Where and how long can I stay in one place? What should I check before buying an RV?

But while there are a lot of questions, a lot of answers are also available. Let's go through all of them.

Things to Check Before Buying an RV

Is the road calling for an adventure? If you answered yes, then an RV might be a great option for your off grid camping. It is, however, essential to remember that buying an RV can be challenging with so many models that are available in the market.

In fact, it is sometimes relatively hard to recognize in a single glance whether the quality of a particular RV is good enough to buy. So before making an investment, here are the factors that you should take a hard look at as you buy an RV.

1. How Will You Use It?

In buying an RV, the first question you should ask yourself is whether you will use it just for camping or for off grid living. Normally, a camping adventure can last for as long as two weeks. It is also essential to consider the number of essentials you are bringing and the people you are traveling with. This is an excellent way to determine what size of RV is ideal for your companions and your budget.

2. Check for Maintenance Records

Maintenance records are without a doubt the most important thing that you should look at before buying an RV. A company or someone who is satisfied with the functionality of their RV will volunteer to show you the maintenance records of the vehicle. By simply examining the maintenance records of an RV, you are able to assure that the vehicle won't cause any problems if you decide to have off-grid camping with your family.

While examining the records, always look for the constancy in oil changes so that you can thoroughly recognize if they were changed regularly and according to the manufacturer's advice. In addition to checking the frequency of oil changes, it is also important to see whether the timing belt has been modified, especially if the vehicle is right within or more than 60,000 miles.

3. Carefully Check for Leaks and Odors

This is especially advisable if you are purchasing a used RV. Always make sure that every component of the vehicle is in order and does not have any issues that might ruin your off grid camping. What I highly recommend is that you inspect the odors, molds, leaks, awnings and the roof of the RV before making a purchase decision.

It would be helpful if you bring someone with you to make sure that nothing is missed during the inspection. Additionally, bring flashlights that will help you examine the rig and the dark spots of the RV.

If your budget is tight, opting for RVs with a few issues can be beneficial on your part (depending on the cost of repairs, of course). Should you feel that there are too many problems and the price is really high, it is best to negotiate with the seller to make sure that you save money in the process.

4. Evaluate the Tires

Looking for wear and tear on tires is imperative, especially if you are planning to purchase a second-hand RV. Regardless of the quality and the wear of the tire, it is optimal for the owner to replace tire once every six years. Tires are extremely expensive if you are driving top-class rigs, and replacing them could cost you an arm and a leg.

One of the quickest ways to examine the quality of the tire is to use your hands to sense ruptures or faults. Apart from scrutinizing the tires in the vehicle, it is also best to inspect the spare tire to ensure that all tires have the same makes and models.

Another easy way to determine the excellence of a tire is by determining its age. You can easily know the age of the tire by simply looking at letters and numbers that are ingrained on their sidewalls. In most cases, a tire has the word "US DOT" along with a four-digit number which indicates the date it was manufactured.

5. Ask For a Test Drive

You have inspected all the parts and everything seems to check your list. Now, one thing must be done and that is asking the seller for a test drive. A test drive will allow you to get the feel of the RV on the road and your ability to drive it with ease and precision.

Drive the RV on open roads (especially if you are driving it for the first time) in order to see how it can handle various speeds as well as braking and turning. It is best to carefully listen for things that are bouncing or shaking when the RV moves. It is, however, crucial to note that the RV you go for a test drive is likely light in weight and will be heavier once you bring in your personal possessions.

Naturally, you don't have to buy an RV right away. Maybe you want to test first whether an RV life is good for you. Maybe you want to check a specific RV model before deciding to purchase it. In such cases, get a rental RV.

RV Features That Really Matter

In choosing an RV, functionality and the home feeling it gives off are among the things that should be taken into serious consideration. Here are features that every RV should have.

1. Water Tanks

Water tanks normally vary according to the size of an RV. It is always super important to go for an RV with water tanks that can easily be connected to outside water systems. This way, you can get fresh and consistent water supply, especially if you are living in off grid trailers.

Cleaning and using disinfectants on water tanks are perhaps the most important aspect of your RV water system maintenance. Always see to it that waste water or black water are distributed in pipes that are opposite to your drinking water, to avoid illnesses and deadly diseases.

2. Bathroom

Having a bathroom is one of the biggest benefits of RV travel. Majority of off-grid trailers come with a decent bathroom that has a toilet you can shower and sit on. While they don't take much so space, smaller RV bathrooms are normally cramped in a small space and everything in the room will essentially get wet.

If you want good-sized bathrooms, it is always recommended

to go after large RVs since it has a small bathtub or stand-up shower as well as a separate toilet and a sink in it.

3. Electricity

Once upon a time, a typical camper did not have an electricity. I doubt that such a setup can work for everyone nowadays. Most of the RVs now have some sort of an electricity source. For instance, a big DC battery. Many campsites provide you with AC electricity via hookups, so RV manufacturers added AC/DC converters, and now you can charge your battery and have a pleasant stay inside.

But if your RV is equipped with all sorts of appliances, a 12 volt battery might not be enough. A lot of RVs come with a built-in generator. It allows people to travel much further and be independent of electrical hookups. It runs your fridge, your TV, your computer, even your toaster and coffee maker. It's your personal power plant!

Notice that a generator requires fuel, which is usually propane, diesel or gasoline. Therefore, you will need to refill your fuel containers from time to time.

You should also consider getting a portable solar panel to aid your power system.

4. Slide Outs

One of the most attractive features of an RV is slide outs. Ordinarily, a slide out can help expand the size of an RV and make it seem larger than it really is. It is, however, important to keep in mind that slides will dramatically increase the weight of your rig, so it is better to park in a place with a sufficient amount of space to slide them out.

Using a slide out will constantly need regular maintenance. To prolong its condition, it is suggested to use a conditioner twice a year to wash its seals.

5. Kitchen

Off-road trailers also have kitchens that are typically comprised of a fridge, a nice sink and a wide range of cooking appliances. A great RV kitchen will also feature a cabinet where you can put your dishes, cutting boards, cups, Tupperware containers, coffee pots and pans, among others.

More often than not, refrigerators that are found in modern RV systems are operated through electricity and gas. You can also choose to install a small generator in your kitchen if you decide to add a microwave.

6. RV Security

Your RV needs to be secured at night, or when you leave it to hike on foot. Never leave your valuables and your loved ones unprotected. Invest into an entry keypad.

7. Basement Storage

Another feature a great RV has is a nice basement storage where you can keep your chairs, carpets, outdoor tables, gears and bicycles. Class A RVs have bigger basement and a much larger storage space as opposed to other types of off-road trailers. There are, however, some class C RVs that have a sizable amount of space for your other utilities as well.

8. Flooring

The flooring of an RV should be customizable based on your likings and preferences. This is an effective way to modernize your RV with an exquisite newly-remodeled look. Often times, removing and replacing the flooring design of your carpet can be completed by yourself in less than no time.

9. Sleeping Area

This just goes without saying. Your home on wheels must

have a bed. Whenever we think of home or even look for a hotel room, the bed is the central piece that turns any four walls into a place suitable for human beings.

Naturally, just a bed is not enough, unless you're on a tight budget. It's especially true in case of a family. What you really need is a bedroom, a space separate from other spaces within the RV. Family RVs often have two or more bedrooms, for parents as well as for children.

I would personally suggest that you also make sure you're getting an RV with a walk-around bed. Unless you want to save on space and get a particularly small RV, this is a must. If it's a bed for two, then every partner will get their own bed approach without the need for hopping over the other's space. This also makes the chore of bed making much easier.

And finally, if you want privacy from the little ones, then your bedroom should be entered through a door and not a curtain. Some RV sellers replace the doors with curtains to make the vehicle lighter. I don't think that you should compromise on your privacy.

10. Seating and Dining Area

This is another significant RV arrangement that completely depends on how many people will be travelling together. Additionally, you might have guests from time to time. Every family member and visitor should have their own seat for dining and relaxation. Consider these factors and then decide on size, quantity and arrangement of the seating places. If you install a TV or a video game console, see whether the seats are facing the entertainment center properly.

How to Start Living in an Off Grid RV

1. Scout the Location

Your first decision should be the location. The beauty of an RV is that you have the freedom of mobility. You can always find a parking spot or a campsite where you spend a night or two, and then drive on to another destination. There are public lands across the USA, where you can live park for free, although I do believe that they are limited to 14 days stay. I discussed free parking spaces in the previous chapter about the self-contained RV. There is also the option of purchasing your own property, where your vehicle can be parked indefinitely.

After you decide where you are going to park, research the weather of the nearby region. What's it like there at nights? Cold, or hot, or humid nights can negatively affect sleeping outdoors in an RV. Then of course, modern RVs come with a great wall isolation, air conditioning, heaters, and so on. Still, decide whether the local climate is going to suit your preferences. Not everyone likes and tolerates every possible weather.

Find the location of important nearby facilities. You would need to locate all necessary buildings, such as a market and a medical facility. Additionally, if you don't want to spend 24 hours in the RV and want a break from exploring the nature, see what entertainment is offered by the current area: movie and regular theaters, restaurants, amusement parks, and so on.

2. Prepare Your RV

As you prepare to live off the grid, take a good look at your RV and decide what tools and equipment it needs before you head for the road. Utensils, plates, fixing tools, electric appliances, and so forth. Do you have a carpet? Then you should get a vaccuum cleaner. Wood flooring? Pack a broom. Make a thorough shopping list, and don't leave for the road until you've crossed out all the items.

Additionally, check your RV's facilities. Does the water tank need to be replenished with fresh water? Maybe it needs some chlorine for additional purification. Was the sewer tank emptied? If not, visit a dumping station as you drive out. Check the propane tanks and fill them, if necessary. And certainly recharge all RV batteries.

After all of this is done, you are ready to go.

3. Settle and Establish Routines

Once you've arrived to your selected location, test various ways to park, so that you fully use the light and the shade of this place. If it's your permanent property, consider making a pad for the RV to stand on. If there are people living nearby, see if you can make some new friends, they can have a lot of useful information about this area.

Establish routines that will keep your RV and its facilities in top shape. Regularly check oil, tires, gas, et cetera, just like you do with a regular car. Create a schedule and commit to it: regularly empty the sewer, refill water and propane, buy groceries.

If you intend to leave after a while, make sure you leave the area pristine clean. We don't want any negative impact on the environment. Repeat steps 1 and 2 and be on your way to freedom.

Can You Fully Live Off the Grid in an RV?

This is a question that deserves a special attention. Let's assume that at this point you've chosen the right RV, got all the necessary tools and equipment, and are now on the road. You are parking whenever you can and living a rent-free, power grid-free life. But can you be 100% off the grid?

The short answer is that with a great, modern RV it is possible. However, there are some extra steps that you need to take.

Most of RVs are, of course, suitable for dry camping. Which means you can travel without relying on hookups. This is also known as boondocking. A typical RV, as explained earlier in the chapter, comes with a water tank, a waste holding tank and even a generator or batteries. Nonetheless, these vehicles are not always designed for people who intend to go off the grid for an extended period of time. Which means that upgrading is in order.

For instance, a lot of RVs include a nice generator, which makes electricity without the need of connecting to a power grid. But you still need the propane to run it. I would suggest upgrading your electricity source by positioning a few solar panels outside your motorhome.

Bear in mind that some contact with the civilization is unavoidable. You will need to periodically visit a nearby town, buy new food, get new water into the tank, empty the waste tank, get rid of the trash, replace broken tools or parts, and so on. But if you conserve water correctly and make an exhaustive shopping list, then you can stay in the wild for even longer. The cost of living off the grid can be reduced if you're being smart with your expenses.

I've also mentioned the issue of the climate. If you wish to stay longer away from humanity, make sure that your RV can handle all seasons. An RV with a good insulation can save you a lot of trouble, as long as it can withstand weather swings. Additionally, consider being on the move when the seasons change, preferably travelling to areas with a comfortable temperature. This way you will save the resources that are usually spent on running the AC and the heaters.

By taking all these additional steps and being wise with your RV maintenance and supplies, a true off the grid experience can be reached. I only ask that you don't damage and pollute your surroundings. Don't start a forest fire, don't leave trash lying around, and in general minimize your impact on the environment. That is the true meaning of being off the grid.

LIVING OFF THE GRID IN A VAN

More and more people decide to leave the "regular" life behind and try living in a van, as they enjoy the open roads and the incomparable sense of freedom. It may sound as if you're sacrificing a lot and that it is difficult to start living inside a van, but it is much easier than you may think.

Is it possible? Is it comfortable? Are you missing anything by living in a van? In this chapter, we will try to answer these and other questions, so let's get into it.

How to Find a Good Park Up Spot and Other Tips

So, you're either thinking about starting off grid living in a van, or you've already decided about it. One of the first things you have to do is to think about a spot to park your van or camper. Living in a van means you can drive and live anywhere you want, and park (almost) anywhere. This may change from place to place and from city to city, so if you decide to park your van in a city, here are a few tips you should follow:

- **Quiet spot**: You would want to choose a place that is quiet and there are no people walking around you at nighttime. Therefore, do not park outside a business that is open for 24 hours or has a 24-hour security.
- **Search online**: The Internet is a useful resource. Use a website like Parkopedia to search for parking lots and garages near you.
- **Several spots**: Choose several spots to park your van,

so that you won't park at the same spot all the time. If you keep parking at the same place and people there do not know you, it may raise suspicion. People may call security or the police on you. When you park at several places, people don't notice you that easily.

- **Camping sites**: You can park your van in dedicated camp sites without worrying about any legal issues or troubles.
- **Truck stops and rest areas**: Usually, truck stops and rest areas will allow you to park your van overnight.
- **City side streets and parks**: There will be times when you'll have to park your van in a city. You can try the parks and side streets, but be aware you're not disturbing anyone or breaking any laws. Simply try to blend in. Always park where it is legal or where local authorities accept presence of those living in their vans.
- **Wheel clamp**: You should put a wheel clamp on the tire, no matter if you're inside your van or not.
- **Blackout curtains**: Blackout curtains are perfect when you choose to live in a van. It allows you to turn the lights on inside the van. This way, no one on the outside will even notice there is anyone in the van.

If you can park your van in a field or a farm, the tips above are not that crucial, but can still be applied. The tips above are mandatory if you decide to park in a city, so you won't disturb other people and won't draw any unnecessary attention.

Solar and Electronics

Charging laptops, cellphones and other electronic devices are possible even if you live off the grid in a van. You can use **12-volt batteries** which will charge your fridge, TV, laptop, cellphone and other devices and appliances. As a result, you can enjoy the life in a van just like in a regular home.

Using two 220Ah batteries, you can charge the following useful appliances:

- Laptop
- Water pump
- Extractor fan
- Sound system
- Lights
- Fridge

You can also use the batteries for chargers, to charge such devices as:

- iPod
- Camera
- Cell phone

For this purpose, you will need a pure sine inverter.

In order to **charge the batteries**, you will need to install solar panels that use the sun's energy to power up the appliances and devices inside your van. I recommend installing two **100W solar panels** on the roof of the van, and these will supply free energy power for everything in your van. You can also use a portable solar panel, which is an extremely useful invention.

But what would you do if it's a cloudy or rainy day, and the sun's rays are not strong enough for your panels? In this case, use a split charge relay. This means that your batteries keep on charging whenever the van's engine is on. This works whether your van is on the move or stationary. When the engine is on, it will charge up your batteries to give you the electric juice.

Charging Different Devices

Different appliances require different sockets in order to charge them. If you wish to charge a cellphone or a USB, a 12V socket it enough. However, if you need to charge your laptop or an appliance such as a food processor, you will require an **inverter**.

These inverters come in various sizes as well as power ratings. They basically convert the power in your 12V batteries into the 240V you are familiar with from home. Know how much power each device needs and how to charge it in order to be prepared.

How to Shower While Living in a Van

Now that you know where to park your car and how to charge your electronic devices and appliances, it's time to get some ideas on how and where to wash up and shower.

Showering in Natural and Outdoor Water Sources

If you live off the grid in a van, then you're probably spending 80% of the time outside. So, one option to shower and clean yourself is by taking advantage of the outdoors and **natural water sources**. Lakes, rivers and waterfalls are great options not only to shower and clean up, but also to connect to Mother Nature.

Another option is using the different **beaches** across the United States, as many of them are equipped with showers. If you plan to use soap and shampoo, make sure it's eco-friendly in order not to harm the environment, the plants and animals.

Rinse Kit

If you're looking for a real proper shower, then you should consider getting a **rinse kit**. It is a portable outdoor camping shower which allows you to enjoy the proper shower that you crave even when living off the grid in a van.

Simply fill the kit with water and enjoy a shower outside of your van. You can also have solar shower bags, as they are very affordable these days and allow you to enjoy **warm and hot showers**. All you have to do is fill the bag with water and let it warm up in the sun. Then, hang the bag up on the van or a nearby tree and enjoy a warm shower outdoors.

24-Hour Gym

Another interesting option (as weird as it may sound) is to get a membership at a gym that is working 24 hours and has shower facilities. This way, you can wash up and use the showers whenever needed, and maybe even stay in shape at the same time.

How to Wash Your Clothes

Scrubba Wash Bag

As for washing and drying your clothes, consider purchasing a product like Scrubba Wash Bag, a pocket-sized portable laundry system. This wash bag is waterproof and comes with a ridged washboard inside.

You simply put your clothes in the bag, add water and some washing powder or gel, seal the bag and scrub the clothes real good. Then, rinse the clothes, squeeze them and hang them to dry in the sun. No electricity required. This amazing invention is widely used by the military.

Knowing People

Another option (although not available at all times) is get to know some good-hearted people or **befriend with people** who are willing to give you access to their washing and drying machines.

How to Drink Water

When you live off the grid in a van, the water issue is approached differently than in a case of living off the grid in a stationary home. At home you can have an access to various water sources, such as a well, a stream, a bore hole or a rain-collecting system. Because you are living in a van and always on the move, you will probably need to install a water filtration system to enjoy clear and clean drinking water.

How does it work? Water filtration system allows you to fill up your water tank with water from any lake and stream, and enjoy safe and clean water for drinking. On the other hand, such a system may be a bit costly.

You can add water to your water tank and without installing a filtration system. But if you would want to drink from that water, you will need to purify it in some way.

Food and Cooking

When you're living off the grid in a van, you save a lot of money. Therefore, you can consume large variety of products. You can drive or walk to the nearest supermarket and purchase a food that you desire at the moment, or you can have a **meal plan**.

What is a meal plan? A meal plan is purchasing only what you need once a week. This way, you avoid getting too much food which will go bad and then to waste. Also, do not forget that you need to plan the space in your van smartly and not stock it with unnecessary products.

Also remember that you need water in order to cook, so create an easy-to-access water system whenever you need water for your cooking. You can also use free water from gyms, outdoor taps, graveyards, friends' houses and so on.

Heating and How to Stay Warm

A reliable heating source allows you to keep warm even inside your van. This ranges from hot water bottles to coal fires. Living off the grid means that you have to provide yourself with the heating source, gas and electric provider. Nonetheless, it is quite possible to keep your van warm enough.

One great option to warm your van is to install a **wood-burner**. It will keep you warm inside your van even when it's freezing cold outside. Wood and coal are easy and cheap to get, so this shouldn't be a problem.

A diesel air heater is also a recommended option. It usually does not consume that much power and fuel, and so it can operate for extended periods of time. More than that, it's really quiet, which allows a deep and comfortable sleep. It's also compact and can easily fit in any van.

How to Use the Toilet

Disposal of waste can be a bit challenging when you live off the grid, especially in a van that is always on the move. You have several options for when you have to use the toilet, so let's review them.

Porta Poti, Nature and Public Toilets

Sure, not the most convenient option to use when you have to go, but when living in a van, it's still a practical solution. Going in the nature or using public toilets is nothing to be ashamed of. However, aside from being a bit uncomfortable, this option still makes you rely on the grid.

Composting Toilet

This is probably the best option for you when you live in a van. Consider installing a composting toilet in your van. It takes the waste and turns it into soil. You can then take this soil and return it to nature, thus fertilizing the ground.

The composting toilet doesn't require any chemicals or water in order to operate. This makes it even friendlier toward the nature and the environment. You also don't need to empty it after every use.

How to Use the Internet

Free Internet

There is a free Internet in abundance anywhere you go, especially in the urban areas. You can park a van in a public place, turn on your phone or laptop and get free connection from most of the nearby business places, such as:

- Restaurants
- Diners
- Coffee shops
- Hotels
- Gyms
- Shopping centers, and so on.

Some of them are password-protected, but for a price of a small espresso you can get the password from a waiter. Alternatively, you can use a website such as Wi-Fi Map that scans for free hotspots in your vicinity.

Paid Internet

If you don't want to rely on the "kindness of the strangers" or chase for free hotspots across the town, try a paid solution. There are quite a few off grid Internet options, which include:

- Satellite Internet
- Ham radio Internet
- Unlimitedville
- Cell phone Internet

All of them require a more detailed explanation, which I invite you to read in my chapter about off grid Internet.

Safety

Safety may be a given when living in a home. But when you live in a van, it's crucial to stay alert and keep safe while stationary or on the road. Here are a few bullet points to consider regarding safe living in a van:

- Always close all doors of the van, especially if you're currently living off the gird in a city.
- Be aware and keep touch with the area and the surroundings.
- Do not park your van in places that may be dangerous

and unsafe.

- Remember risks of natural disasters, stay protected and safe at all times.

How to Earn Money While Living in a Van

There are a lot of creative ways to earn money even when you are living in a van. Here are some of the possible options to consider:

- **Working remotely**: Work from home (or the van in this case) is very much possible. You can find jobs on Fiverr, Upwork, or even become an Internet marketer, promoting products and services and earning commissions. You will most likely need to have a laptop and an Internet access. The jobs can range from content writing to graphic design, to coding jobs, to data entry, and so on.
- **Temp agency work**: Temp agencies offer people opportunities to earn money on jobs that are short term. If you are skilled, chances are big that you'll score a decent temp job.
- **Seasonal jobs**: You can find seasonal farm jobs all across the United States. Construction season can provide jobs to earn money, as well as commercial fishing seasons. In Western U.S., you may even find a seasonal job with crews that fight wildfires.
- **Delivery jobs**: You can work as a delivery person for companies like Amazon, Wal-Mart and Uber. You may need to own a bike or a car in order to make these deliveries, as you won't be doing them with your van.
- **Use your own skills**: Be creative! If you possess different skills or have knowledge that can be useful, advertise and offer your skills and knowledge on Facebook and Craigslist.

LIVING OFF THE GRID IN THE CITY

Imagine this scenario. You live in the middle of the city, everything is in reach, yet you are free of urban infrastructures, self-sufficient and dependent just on yourself. Oh, and you save a lot of money in the long run, too. Does that sound like something you wish to achieve?

I have talked a lot in this book about off grid living, but was concentrating on living in a remote area, alone or with a community, but basically outside the city. Now, I would like to cover this subject from another point of view: how to enjoy all the benefits of living off the grid, while staying in the city, in a close proximity to everything you know and love.

So, let's cover this subject and see how you can live off the grid in the city and stay close to friends, family and everything else you've been accustomed to.

Benefits of Living off the Grid in the City

Aside from environmental and mental benefits of living off the grid, I want to focus mostly on the financial benefits, which probably interest you a lot more. So, here are some of the main benefits to consider when deciding to live off the grid in the city:

- You can save 90% of energy as well as water usage in comparison to regular homes. This means that you save a lot of money!
- You can save up to 50% or more when it comes to

households utility bills.

- Start living off the grid and save up to $1,314 per year only on utilities.
- You save a lot of money when you grow your own food (even some of it) instead of purchasing at the store.
- You don't have to care if the power in your neighborhood is out, there's no running water or other problems with the city's infrastructure. You're all self-sufficient, produce and supply for yourself.
- Life becomes less stressful when you're self-sufficient and not dependent on anyone or anything.

Producing Off Grid Electricity

Living off the grid means you'll start producing power and electricity on your own, which will save you a lot of money. If you have surplus power, check with local authorities if you can sell them the power you've stored. This way you can even make money from your own produce.

What are the components required?

- Solar panels
- Battery pack
- Solar inverter
- Battery inverter
- Wiring equipment

I will now cover the main components when it comes to producing your own power source, so you'll have a better idea how this works and how to choose the battery to store the energy. The other components are important as well, but these are the two main ones to elaborate about.

Solar Panels

The easiest and most popular way to generate your own power and electricity is by installing solar panels. The best place to install the panels are on the roof of the house. If this is not possible, you can install them on the ground as well, just make sure they are not near anything that can damage them or fall on them, like trees for example. Also, make sure they are exposed to enough sunlight in order to produce the sufficient energy your household and appliances require.

How does this work you ask? Solar panels contain photovoltaic (pv) cells on their surface and they convert the sunrays to electric direct current (DC). Solar panels contain multiple cells and all of them are linked together. Solar panels are available with mono cell arrangement, half cut cell arrangement, shingled cell arrangement, or busbar cell arrangement. The bottom of the solar panel comes with wire connectors and they transfer the power generated into your house.

Solar panels are rated according to the amount of DC current that they produce after exposing them to sunlight for a period of time. That is why you should purchase solar panels that are able to charge the battery pack fully in one day.

Battery Pack

The battery is extremely important because it stores the energy that you produce. With that energy, you are able to use devices and appliances that require electricity. More than that, because there will be times when there is not enough exposure to sunrays, like during the winter, night-time, when there's a fog and other times when the sunrays are blocked, the energy stored in the battery will allow you to use it in later use. Additionally, the power becomes more stable inside the battery before it reaches electrical appliances.

There are different kinds of batteries to choose from:

- **Lead-Acid batteries**: This type of battery is very durable, it can be used until it almost discharges completely. These batteries will not shut down all of a sudden, as compared to other types of batteries. Moreover, most inverters on the markets are compatible with these batteries, making them my first choice.

- **Lithium ion batteries**: This type of battery is compact and therefore portable. They are light, small, yet have high efficiency. Charging this battery takes less time than charging a lead-acid battery, and there are no worries about sulfation (a more common problem with lead-acid batteries). All this and more makes this battery also ideal for off-grid solar power setups.

Here's the thumb rule for picking a battery to store the power and energy: **pick a battery that can hold enough charge in order to power all the devices and appliances in the house until the next time it needs to be fully charged**. This means that the battery pack must hold enough charge in it to power all equipment in the house overnight, so that the battery can be recharged the following day.

Here are some recommended solar systems to consider:

- **Grape Solar GS-400-Kit Off-Grid Solar Panel Kit**: This is a standalone and fully equipped solar system kit. It comes with four mono-crystalline solar panels that can generate enough energy to power bulbs as well as small electrical devices and equipment. The panels have an included junction box with LED lights that improve the performance of the kit. It also includes a 35-amp charge controller and an inverter with an output rating of 2000 watts. However, bear in mind that the kit does not include a battery pack, so if you want to store power in order to use it later, you need to purchase a battery separately.
- **Astronergy Medium Solar Off-Grid Solar Power System**: This medium-sized solar system kit comes with nine solar panels each having an output rating of 260 watts. It also includes a remote controlled 4400-watt inverter and eight deep cycle batteries that hold

enough charge to power small as well as heavy-duty electric devices and appliances.

- **RENOGY Solar Panel Kit 400W, Off-Grid, with Mounting Brackets**: This kit comes with four 100-watt solar panels. They are rated A for energy efficiency, and sold with Z-shaped brackets that hold the panels at an optimum exposure angle and can be mounted even on a flat surface. The solar panels can also withstand brutal and harsh weather conditions and produce enough power even when sunlight is low. The kit does not include batteries to store power, so purchase them separately.
- **Eco-Worthy 1000W, 10 Pieces, Solar Module for Homes**: This kit comes with 10 100-watt solar panels, generating all together an output of 1000 watts. The kit also includes 10 180-centimetre long solar cables and 10 MC4 extensions. The polycrystalline solar panels have an inbuilt bypass diode that negates the shadow effect on the panels, thus allowing conversion of sunlight into electric power even in low sunlight. The junction box that comes with the panel is waterproof and weather-resistant, so it enables the solar panels to withstand heavy rainfall as well as snow. The heavy gauge aluminum frame surrounding the solar panels also protects them from corrosion.

Getting Off Grid Water in the City

There are different ways to enjoy water supply when living off the grid (digging a well, borehole, etc'), but in the city, the best way to have your own source of water is probably by collecting rainwater. Living in the city, you can save a lot of money in two ways:

1. Build a simple rainwater harvesting system to collect rainwater and store it inside tanks.

2. Use techniques to save water.

Rainwater Harvesting System

Rainwater harvesting system (also known as rainwater catchment system) can range from simple barrels that collect rain to sophisticated systems that use tanks, pumps and advanced filters. The non-potable water can be used to wash the car, flush toilets, landscaping and washing the clothes. Water that was purified is safe to drink and consume.

The simplest harvesting systems for rainwater are non-pressurized systems. These can be rain barrels, where rain gutters and a tank are connected by pipes. These "dry systems" don't hold any water in the pipes after rain has stopped falling, and so don't create breeding grounds for mosquitoes and other insects.

Other systems are known as "wet systems", where the pipes don't run directly into the tanks ebcause such a configuration is not available. When the water tanks are located away from the surfaces collecting the rainwater, pipes from the gutter are placed underground and then go up into the tanks. Most of the times these systems will be pressurized so that the pipes won't retain stagnant water.

A quality rainwater harvesting system will ensure that the pipes and other openings are well proofed against insects. This is highly important in wet systems.

As for the surfaces that collect the rainwater (mostly roofs), they must be made of materials that are not-toxic. Avoid paint that is lead-based and membranes. The tanks that store the water should be made from a material that is non-toxic as well as non-corrosive. The draw-off pipes and outlet pipes must be 4 inches or more above the tank's floor. This is done to ensure that sludge is not being drawn out. Some systems come with washout pipe and sump pump that take care of the sludge. Still, you must regularly clean the inner tank surfaces, no matter how advanced your rainwater harvesting system is.

Also, remember to clean and keep the catchment clean from moss, dirt, lichens and various debris, and cut back tree branches that hang over the catchment surface. Regularly clean the gutters, inlets of the tanks and make a yearly inspection to see that everything works properly.

Now, let's talk about the quality of the water. Rainwater can mix with different materials from the surfaces it lands on, thus collecting pollutants and dust. Contaminants in the water may include fungi, plants, metals, chemicals, dissolved minerals, water-soluble paints, and more. If you wish to use the rainwater for gardening or cleaning, they do not require purity in a high degree. However, they are not suitable for cooking or drinking.

When you separate the first flush of rainwater from the roof, gutters and other surfaces that collect the rainwater, you actually improve and make the quality of the water better and safer to drink. Rainwater for the purposes of household and consumption must be purified.

Water stored in the tanks can get contaminated with bacteria, different chemicals and other organic material that settle on the bottom of the tank as sludge or form films on the surface of the water. You can remove it by processes of settlement, biofilm skimming and flocculation. You can also purify the water with chemicals such as calcium hydroxide, fluoride and potassium permanganate.

Techniques to Save Water

If you prefer to stay connected to the city's pipelines instead of collecting rainwater, that's fine. There are still ways to save water and money. Here are a few techniques to use in order to save water and spend less money living in the city:

- **Cutting shower**: If you cut your shower by 1-minute only, you can save up to $160 per year for a household of four people.
- **Reusing water**: You can reuse the water of the dish

washer and the bathtub in order to water the garden.

- **Fixing dripping tops**
- **Water saving showerhead**: Using a special showerhead in the shower can save you a lot of money when not using too much water.

No More Gas

Instead of using gas, install a wood burning stove. There are different types of burners, but I suggest choosing a new and eco-friendly wood stove burner. This way, you'll reduce emissions of particle by no less than 90% compared to an open fire and 80% compared to a stove that is old.

The cost of the material you need to use in order to burn in the stove is cheaper than using gas. If you can insulate your home well, you will save even more money. The bigger the system, the more you'll be able to use it around the house. You'll be able to cook, heat the water in the boiler, use heating under the floor, secondary heating to room, and more.

Grow Your Own Food in the City

If you have enough space around your house and a room for setting a garden, it's time to think about growing your own food. It's not that difficult, and apart from the food being much tastier than store-bought, you'll be saving a whole lot of money here as well. I won't go over the types of soil that each crop or vegetable requires, so let's assume that your soil is suitable for growing food (naturally, you must ensure that your soil is fertile for you start anything).

Here is what you start growing on your own:

- **Herbs**: Herbs spice up your typical foods and make them taste even better. Apart from them being delicious, they are also healthy and grow easily. It's best to have a separate garden for herbs. Grow different types of herbs by making an herb spiral. It's basically a pile of dirt with stones that spiral down, and this way make a little spiraling ramp.

- **Fruits and vegetables**: Because it can take years to enjoy fruits, you should first plant fruit and nut trees. Set up a berry patch. Because berries are perennial plants, they will come back each and every year. They can be used and eaten when dried, preserved into jams, jellies or frozen.
  As for growing vegetables, they go into three categories: heavy feeders, light feeders, heavy givers. It's important to know that you have to rotate between the groups in order that your soil is never depleted.
  The heavy feeders are asparagus, beet, broccoli, corn, strawberries, and okra. These should be followed by light feeders like garlic, carrot, sweet potato, Swiss chard. These should now be followed by heavy givers like beans, peas, alfalfa, peanuts, clover.
  If the space in your garden is not enough, you should check for community gardens. You can find them in many cities, and you can grow vegetables on their plot for a low cost or even freely. Fruit trees are also great resources for off grid food. Cities and urban areas are filled with them, so you can forage for wild or semi-wild plants, just like in the country.
- **Grains**: Grains are very easy to grow and you don't need many acres to grow them. After you purchase them, spread them in the ground, planting them 6 inches deep. Make sure that this spot gets a lot of sunlight. You can use a seeder to spread the seeds evenly. A seeder is something like a jar with perforated lid. When the crops are ready to be harvested, use something like a hedge trimmer or pruning shears to collect them. Beat the stalks with a stick to loosen the seeds from them. The final stage is freeing the grains from their coating, which can be simply achieved by pour-

ing the grain between two containers before an operating fan. Basically, 1000 feet of soil is enough to get a bushel of wheat, which produces 60 lbs. of grain.

Now, if you have enough room and space, you can even raise livestock. Animals are good at taking care of themselves, if they have the proper environment. Because you live in the city, I will stick to easier livestock to raise, and these will probably be chickens (living away from the city allows you to grow pigs, cows, sheep, ducks, and other animals).

Raising chickens is not difficult at all. They don't take a lot of space and once they have a coop and a piece of land, they are all set. Chickens prefer free range, and can provide you with an egg a day. All they require is fresh water, a good and reliable source of calcium and protein, shelter (to include shade), and a place to take a dust bath. Chicken poop is also a great crop fertilizer. They poop on the ground, and eat the bugs and the grass. When you move them, you have a perfect plot of land to grow in: great fertilizer, no bugs and the grass is gone.

Off Grid Sanitation and Water Waste

This is not a must, but if you're interested living life off the grid, this can be applied to sanitation, meaning you'll be using less water and save more money, again. First, let's understand two main phrases when it comes to off grid sanitation, greywater and blackwater, and then I'll go over 4 different options for off grid sanitation.

- **Greywater**: This is used water from sinks, showers, tubes and washing machines.
- **Blackwater**: This is used water from toilets as well as other sources of water with human waste.

Now, let's go over 4 options for off grid waste water and how to deal with them:

- **Composting toilets**: This is one of the best and most common ways to deal with blackwater when it comes to off grid. Composting toilets take some getting used to, but they are great since you're saving a whole lot of water (and with that money), because there's no flushing involved. These are dry toilets that compost human waste biologically. Therefore, it does not require plumbing or flushing and does not require the use of any chemicals. However, if you decide to use composting toilets along with a septic system, then you actually divert the waste from the tanks and this way extend the system's life.

There are different types of composting: aerobic composting (oxygen is applied to aid in the breaking down of waste material), anaerobic composting (usually takes little effort, if a composter is present), and vermicomposting (involves the usage of worms, moisture, and oxygen to aid in the breaking down of waste material).

Composting toilets usually include a ventilation unit, storage container, access opening and diversion system. Human waste is collected with the same container (or "chamber").

- **Greywater systems**: If you reuse greywater properly, it's a great way to conserve water and resources. Here are a few ways to design your private greywater system at home:

  1. You can purchase a greywater tank and system
  2. Rig different appliances like your shower, which diverts the greywater to the toilets or to outdoor tanks in order to use in the garden.
  3. Create a greywater system on your own from materials you have at home.

- **Lagoons**: Lagoons are utilizes wherever the soil cannot filter effectively. Lagoons are earthen basins. The wastewater is drained into them and processed by microorganisms. They may be very effective, however not always approved. So, before setting or installing one, check to see if you have permission for a lagoon.

- **Septic systems**: Septic systems are the most common systems to deal with waste water. They are also the ones that are easily approved. The wastewater from your home simply drains into a septic tank. Inside the tank, the solids begin to settle at the bottom of the tank and then break down. In the meantime, water gradually filters out through holes in pipes, which are located at the septic drain field.

Off Grid Internet and Communication

If you mustn't be connected to the internet for the purposes of work, streaming or gaming, there is no reason to pay a provider or sign an Internet plan. These days, a lot of places like coffee shops and even public places offer free Wi-Fi. This makes connecting to the Internet easy and free. If you need to use a computer, many Internet cafes and libraries offer logging in to the Internet for free as well.

There are other easy ways you can get online, some are free and some are not, yet they are still cheap. These ways include using cell phone, satellite, private hotspot, ham radio or a service called Unlimitedville. You can read the chapter about off grid Internet where I elaborate about all these ways to get online.

There are also devices that allow you to send messages, share your location, download maps, and so on. They work even if there is no Wi-Fi or satellite signal available. They are used mostly outdoors, during hiking, camping activities and emergencies. If this interests you, I'd like to refer you back to the chapter about off grid communication.

FINAL WORDS

So there you have it, dear reader. I hope this was more than enough information to get you started.

Living off the grid is an adventure and a challenge. With the right mindset and determination, you will be able to overcome whatever obstacles you encounter on your path to personal freedom. I believe in you, and you must believe in yourself, too. You have the undeniable potential to carve your own niche in this gigantic world.

And yes, our world is gigantic, and there is a plenty of room just for you. So load your van, truck or RV, and get away from the stuffy environment that monitors your every step while polluting your air and your water.

I'd wish you good luck on your journey, but luck is not enough. You are now armed with knowledge and can make your own luck. Always remember to never stop learning and expanding your horizons, challenging old preconceptions and gaining tons of experience.

You are now ready to move forward, let go of constrictions and truly be off the grid.

ABOUT THE AUTHOR

Alexander Rejba

Alexander Rejba is the author of The Smart Survivalist website. He is passionate about survival skills and challenges, off-the-grid living, hiking, camping and science fiction.
If you have any feedback or questions regarding this book or any other upcoming books and projects, feel free to contact him at https://www.TheSmartSurvivalist.com